The Valley of the Queens

Châteaux of the Loire
From the Indre to the Loire

The Valley of the Queens

Châteaux of the Loire
From the Indre to the Loire

FRANÇOIS COLLOMBET

PHOTOGRAPHS
PASCAL LEMAÎTRE
AND
DAVID BORDES

TRANSLATION
CHRISTOPHER THIERY

Les Éditions du Huitième Jour

CONTENTS

9 — **GIEN** — Madame la Grande

13 — **SULLY** — A guest for the duke

19 — **BEAUGENCY** — Without doubt the woman of the century

23 — **TALCY** — Mignonne, allons voir si la rose

29 — **CHAMBORD** — The most beautiful of learned ladies

43 — **VILLESAVIN** — Two women in charge

49 — **BLOIS** — The three queens

63 — **BEAUREGARD** — Anne, Diane, Catherine and the others

67 — **CHEVERNY** — Love story

73 — **CHAUMONT** — The "Empress of the mind"

83 — **AMBOISE** — A young queen and a festive woman

93 — **LE CLOS-LUCÉ** — The mysterious Florentine lady

97 — **CHENONCEAU** — A token of love

109 — **SAINT-AIGNAN** — The Scandalous Woman

113 — **MONTPOUPON** — She rode side-saddle

117 — **MONTRÉSOR** — Bunia Branicka

THE LOIRE FROM QUEEN TO QUEEN

Anna Branicka - Solange de la Motte Saint Pierre - Jeanne de Perellos - Diane de Poitiers - Mona Lisa - Anne de Bretagne - Madame de Staë

In the year 2000 the Loire valley became the second French cultural site included on the prestigious UNESCO World Heritage List. The "Valley of the Queens", shaped by the Loire, is a unique journey through history. Observe the river in summer, as it dawdles in a bed decidedly too wide for it. See how it meanders gently among the sandbanks and the smooth stones. In the heat of summer, after such strenuous effort, it turns into a silver stream sliding along the banks made golden by the sun, dallying among

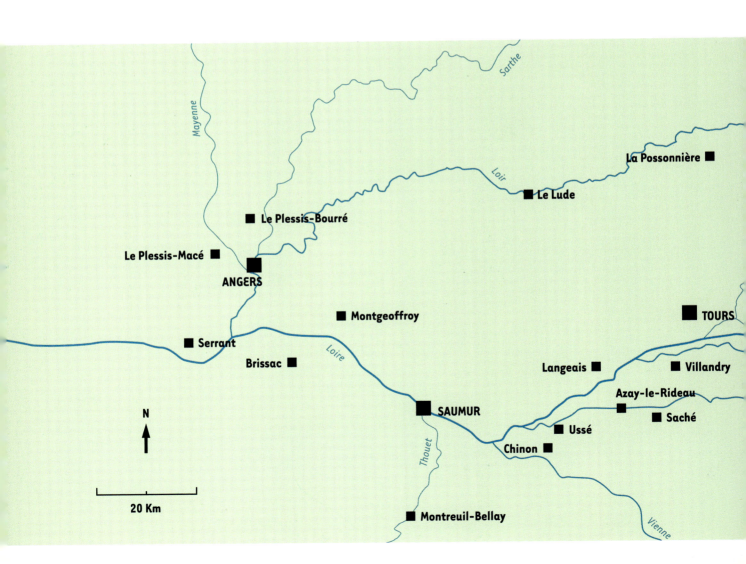

arguerite - Marie de Medicis - Anne de Pisseleu - Cassandre - Aliénor d'Aquitaine - Jeanne d'Arc - Anne de Beaujeu

the streams and the rivers that flow into it: the Cher, the Indre, the Vienne, and even the respectful Loir that accompanies the royal river at a suitable distance… From Gien to Angers the Loire mingles periods and styles. It will be your guide through nine centuries of history, leading you from Queen to Queen. Whether they were queens or regents, women of war or of letters, women of yesterday or of today, they are truly the souls of these châteaux.

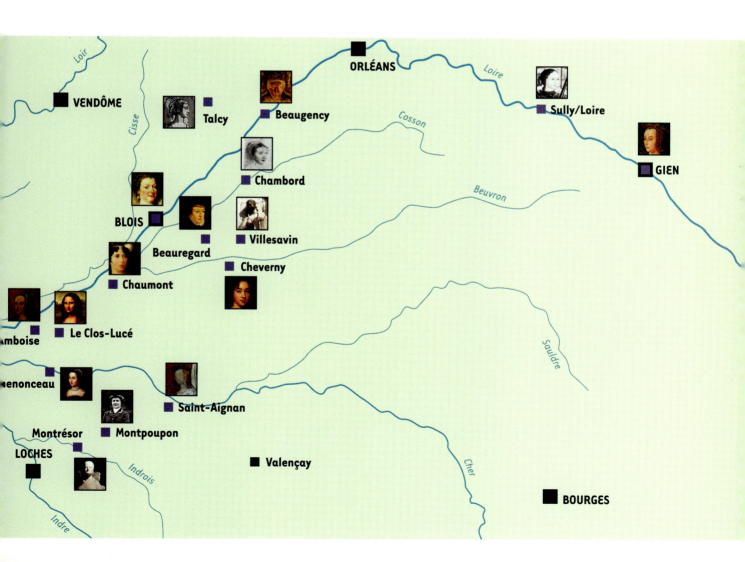

Anne de Beaujeu

Madame la Grande: Gien

November 1484: Anne de Beaujeu, Countess of Gien and Regent of the Kingdom, was at the height of her power. She had recently succeeded both in removing the least popular advisors of Louis XI, her recently deceased father, and at convening the States General. The "parliament" confirmed her regency and her 14-year-old brother, King Charles VIII, would be under her tutelage. He was by her side to witness the beginning of the construction of the bridge at Gien, the very same bridge that is used to cross the Loire today. Construction of the castle wasn't begun until 10 years after the bridge was finished.

The first château of the Loire

The site is exceptional. In Gallo-Roman times a stronghold had already been built on this limestone promontory above the Loire. Charlemagne consolidated it in order to protect the country from the Barbarian invasions. In 1178 Louis VII the Young dismantled the fortress for the first time. It was however Anne de Beaujeu, eldest daughter of Louis XI, who in the 15th century turned the excessively military, defensive structure into a pleasant place to live in.

Right-hand page:
The tower of the château's east staircase.

Below:
Over 500 trophies are exhibited in the museum.

The "least mad woman of the kingdom"

Anne of France, known as the Dame de Beaujeu after having married Pierre de Beaujeu, Duke of Bourbon, shared with her father, Louis XI, an ugly face and an acute sense of politics. "She is the least mad woman in France, for of wise women, I know none" he used to say of her. So when he felt his death was nigh, (he died on 31 August 1483), he entrusted her with the regency of the kingdom, on behalf of her young brother Charles VIII. She had complete control over the Government Council set up to assist the young sovereign. Had she not just convened the States General without giving up the slightest royal prerogative?
When, in 1494, she undertook the construction of the château of Gien, she was no more at the height of her power.
For Gien, these were the finest times in its history. Gien owes a lot to Anne de Beaujeu: the château church, the Minimes convent, (now a porcelain factory), the St Lazare chapel, the Clarisse convent, and the famous bridge.

A place of refuge during the Fronde uprising

In 1652, when the Fronde uprising was gathering momentum in Paris, challenging Richelieu and the monarchy, the château of Gien served as a place of refuge for the young Louis XIV, then aged 14, and his mother Anne of Austria, accompanied by Mazarin. The king was supposed to inspect the troops of the royal Austrian army, entrenched in Gien. Nothing was ready for receiving the royal visitors. The king's valet, Pierre de la Porte, complained that the king had nothing to wear: "For three years, all he had for summer and winter was a green velvet dressing-gown which barely reached below the knees." (He had outgrown it!) The Fronde troops, under Condé, were beaten by Turenne, who received a hero's welcome at Gien on the part of the king and the court.
After being damaged in 1940, the château of Gien was restored and now houses the magnificent International Hunting Museum.

tour

A black-and-red brick mosaic

The château consists of three buildings set at right angles, with the white stone frames contrasting with the red-and-black bricks set in a diamond formation.
Trying to catch a glimpse of the enigmatic figures on the north and west walls of the room at the top of the stair tower, is worth the effort. Composed in brick, they lend themselves to somewhat esoteric interpretations.
A square upper room accessible by stair curiously caps the polygonal tower. It was the custom in the late 14th and early 15th century to build rooms at the top of staircases. They were small rooms that projected slightly, and were lived in, as is seen by the presence of a fireplace.

The International Hunting Museum

Gien is at the heart of one of the finest hunting regions of France, and is called "the capital of hunting".
The château is entirely given over to hunting and the history of hunting weapons since prehistoric times. Over 3,000 objects and works of art, displayed in fourteen rooms, illustrate the techniques and customs of hunting over the centuries.
There are ancient firearms, such as Napoleon's double-barrelled flint gun, and General Cambronne's shotgun.

There are also works of art with hunting themes, such as the animal paintings by Louis XIV's hunting artist, François Desportes (1661-1743), which are displayed in the impressive hall with the beautiful beamed ceiling on the first floor.
The museum also boasts an exceptional collection of over 4,000 hunting buttons and horns, as well as Mr Hétier de Boislanbert's 500 personal trophies, and those of Mr François de Grossouvre

Joan of Arc

A guest for the duke: Sully

March 1430: Was Joan of Arc a guest of the Duke de la Trémoille at Sully? Hardly. Under house arrest would be closer to the truth, for the Maid had become something of an embarrassment to the king. At La Trémoille's suggestion, Charles VII had decided to improve relations with his enemy, the Duke of Burgundy, allied to the English. Joan was against the idea, so La Trémoille planned to have her assassinated in his chateau in Sully. By several accounts, one of his men was to push her over the wall during a stroll along the sentry walk. Did she sense the danger? In any event, on 28 March 1430 she left Sully in great haste, "without the king's knowledge and without so much as a by-your-leave".

Drawn up by the king's architect

According to some historians, Sully was already a fort in Gallo-Roman times. In 1381 the castle became the property of the Lords of la Trémoille. Guy de la Trémoille and his wife, Marie de Sully, undertook to construct a keep, based on plans – revolutionary for their time – drawn up by the king's celebrated architect, Raymond du Temple (he was also renovating the Louvre). It would be a rectangular keep with a round tower at each of the four corners, and a gateway with two towers, facing south.

Above: The native château of Sully, in Rosny-sur-Seine.

The great Sully in his château

The most famous occupant was certainly Maximilien de Béthune (1560-1641), Baron of Rosny, by his real name. He was a great soldier and statesman, and he left his mark not only on the kingdom, but also on his château. His ministerial responsibilities included Finance, Agriculture, Industry and Public Works, and despite being a Protestant he was made a duke. When being told so, he is supposed to have said to Henry IV: "Your Majesty, I would be a happy Duke if the estate closest to my heart, Sully, could be attached to my new title." His career came to end in 1610 with Henri IV's assassination.

He devoted the last thirty years of his life to embellishing the château and was responsible for its only Renaissance flourishes. He restored and enlarged the original fortress, strengthened the embankments to protect it and the town from the Loire's floods, put in slate roofs, and opened up tall windows overlooking the moat. He also built the Béthune tower, which housed his famous study, and designed the park. The château remained in his descendants' possession for four centuries after his death.

DUKE AND AUTHOR

From 1611 to 1617 Sully worked on his memoirs in his château. They were called "Memoirs of the wise and royal policies of the State in the domestic, political and military affairs of Henry the Great." He rose each day at 3 and wrote all morning long, with four secretaries to assist him. For the sake of convenience he had a printing press brought in from Angers. The operation cost 5,223 livres, a paltry amount compared to the vast fortune he had made.

Voltaire at Sully

It wasn't until the 18th century that the Age of Enlightenment finally reached Sully, in the person of Voltaire. The exile of the young Arouet included some libertine pursuits, but at 22 the budding philosopher was already much admired and also much applauded for his sentimental imbroglios, on and off the stage. In 1774 the ninth duke had the foresight to have the tops of the towers removed, to avoid provoking the revolutionaries. This precaution was to no avail, however. The château was ransacked all the same, and after the Revolution it was abandoned and fell into ruin.

In 1900 a Béthune restored it, but there was a fire in 1918, and it suffered heavily from the terrible bombings of 1940 and 1944. In view of the enormous repairs required, the owner put it up for sale in 1961. After a bitterly contested auction, Sully was sold for 654,210 francs. The Loiret Department has since restored it.

tour

An impregnable edifice

The château of Sully, not far from the basilica St Benoît on the other side of the river, seems somewhat incongruous in the Loire valley, which is so marked by the Renaissance. For Sully is clearly a defensive structure, with its massive rectangular keep facing the river and the impressive height of the roof. Sully stands in what is really a small lake, formed by the Sange, a minor affluent of the Loire. In the Middle Ages, access was by a drawbridge, the Priests' bridge, an exact replica of which was rebuilt in 1994. There are two periods at Sully: the vieux (old) château, dating from the 14th century, mainly a defensive structure, and the petit (little) château, built by Sully in the 17th century.

The vieux château

The vieux château, facing the Loire, is a rectangular keep with four round towers at the corners and a machicolated sentry walk. This was a remarkable innovation, making it possible to move rapidly from one part of the château to another. A garrison of fifteen men was thus sufficient to defend the fortress.
The oak frame of the keep, dating from the 14th century, is a masterpiece of perfection. As soon as the trees were felled, the logs were immersed in water for many months in order to rid them of sap. Later, after being dried and smoke-cured, they were washed in an alum solution to proof them against rot. On the ground floor large windows put in by Sully light the guardroom, with its six-metre-high ceiling. On the first floor is a large room where Voltaire staged his plays.

The petit château

The petit château is the Renaissance pavilion where Sully had his study. The minister's bedroom is on the first floor; his motto, *À moi Béthune*, ("Béthune is mine") is inscribed on the chimney-piece. There are some fine tapestries and hangings, in particular a series of six monumental 17th-century tapestries representing Psyche

*Left-hand page:
The superb 14th-century
timber frame.*

Eleanor of Aquitaine

Without doubt the woman of the century: Beaugency

Since their return from the Crusades, Louis VII, the King of France, and Eleanor of Aquitaine, the Queen, had been at loggerheads. The only person who might have reconciled them was Suger, the abbot of St Denis, but he had died year earlier. In 1152 the Council of Beaugency annulled their marriage, "for reasons of consanguinity". The real reason was that the exuberant Eleanor could no longer stand her timorous husband, who was steeped in piety. Six months later she married Henry Plantagenet, Count of Anjou, future King of England. Her dowry included the territories of Gascony, Poitou, Saintonge, Limousin, Angoumois and Perigord.

What was left for the dauphin?

This annulment had devastating consequences for the French crown, which lost, a third of its territory. When in 1328 the King of France, Charles IV the Fair, died, without leaving a son, Edward II of England claimed the crown as the grandson, through his mother, of Philip the Fair, thereby starting a war that was to last a hundred years…

Below:
The château has been turned into the displaying regional furnishings.

The situation was summed up in a popular song. "What is there left for the sweet dauphin: Orleans, Beaugency, Notre-Dame de Cléry, Vendôme, Vendôme…" And in 1429 that was indeed all that was left to the sweet dauphin, the young Charles VII: a popular ditty and the paltry remains of a kingdom. The English, led by the Duke of Bedford, were the lords of the land. They held Beaugency and its bridge; with its twenty arches it was the only way of crossing the Loire between Orleans and Blois.

What had the English to fear, safe inside the big rectangular keep at Beaugency? It had been built in the 11th century by Fulk Nerra, at the same time as Loches, and was considered at the time to be a masterpiece of the art of defence.

As for the young Charles VII, he had every reason to doubt: about his filiation and about his crown… and then Joan of Arc, a peasant girl just 17 years old, recognised him amidst the crowd of anonymous courtiers at Chinon, and thanks to her, hope was rekindled.

The fall of Beaugency

On 8 May 1429 Joan of Arc, at the head of her troops, delivered Orleans by surprise. Her progression was then a long series of battles. On 15 June, Meung was taken, Jargeau abandoned. On 18 June, Beaugency fell for the fourth time, before the decisive victory of Patay. Suffolk was captured and the Loire was freed. Auxerre, Troyes and Chalons were further victories on the road to Reims, where Charles VII was crowned on 17 July 1429.

The present château of Beaugency was fitted out by Dunois, one of Joan of Arc's companions and an illegitimate son of the Duke of Orleans. In 1440 he put up a two-storey building with a stair tower and a courtyard. He lived there for seven years, until Chateaudun was finished.

The Department bought the château in the 19th century to provide shelter for the homeless.

The rectangular 11th-century keep.
Originally it had five storeys and was 36 metres in height.

tour

The best way to see Beaugency for the first time is from the 15th-century bridge, at the time the only one between Blois and Orleans. The English and the French fought for it endlessly throughout the Hundred Years' War. The town is situated on the right-hand bank of the Loire, and has developed around the château and the abbey since the Middle Ages.

The rectangular 11th-century keep, with its flat buttresses, is 36-metres tall and still towers over the town. Initially it had five storeys, but when the Huguenots set fire to it in 1567 the roof was destroyed.

The Dunois château was fitted out in 1440 in the old fortress belonging to the Lord of Beaugency. It is typical of 15th-century residences, with its mullioned windows, enclosed courtyard and private garden.

In the 16th century Dunois's descendants added the spiral staircase and the Longueville wing. The impressive 15th-century attic timber frame, shaped like a ship's hull, is definitely worth a look. In 1928 the Department opened the Orleans Regional Museum in the château. Quite recently the Historical Monuments Authority has reconstituted a medieval garden, on the basis of documents and miniatures dating from Dunois's time. The fountain and geometrically laid-out plots of aromatic and medicinal plants give an idea of what a 15th-century garden was like.

Cassandra

Mignonne, allons voir si la rose...
Talcy

Never have the ladies of a château inspired so many poets. First it was the very beautiful Cassandra Salviati: "Mignonne, let us see if the rose, That this morning did expose, Her purple robe to the sun..." She was the rose! He had met her at Blois, at a ball given by François I. She was 16, and he, Pierre de Ronsard, was twenty-one. It was passionate, but unrequited love. Leaning against the well, in the fragrance of the rose bush on a summer's evening, the poet sang of his lost loves: "If such a flower lasts only till day is out, gather, gather in your youth, For like the rose your beauty will be dulled by age".

A Florentine merchant

Bernardo Salviati was a Florentine merchant belonging to a family allied to the Medicis, and like many Italians of the early Renaissance, he came to live on the banks of the Loire. In all likelihood he was banker to François I. At any event, on 8 November 1517 he purchased the "land, estate and seigniory of Talcy". It was an old 12th-century estate belonging to the Simons, a family of Parisian magistrates.

On 12 September 1520 Salviati was authorised by the Lord of Beaugency to build a "maison forte". What an anachronism! In the early 16th century, at a time when the Renaissance was drastically changing architecture in the Loire valley, Bernardo Salviati wanted to make Talcy a purely Gothic edifice with "moats, chained drawbridges, loopholes, barbicans and several other forms of defence". In actual fact he kept only the medieval keep, in which he put mullioned windows. There was never the slightest drawbridge or moat. He married Françoise Doucet, and had four children. One of them was Cassandra, born in 1530.

In the spring of 1545 a ball was given at the château of Blois. Like the Salviatis, Pierre de Ronsard, who lived at Vendôme, was invited. The poet only had eyes for the beautiful Cassandra Salviati. "I saw her, and fell madly in love" he declared. So smitten was he that even seven years later his anthology of love poems, *Les Amours de Cassandre*, was dedicated to her. But love does not pay the rent. Poor Ronsard was only a poet, and Bernardo Salviati had other ambitions for his daughter. The following year she was married to Jean de Pray.

From poet to poet

A few decades later, another poet wooed another young Salviati at Talcy: Cassandra's niece Diana. Agrippa d'Aubigné (1552-1630) was Henri IV's companion, and much admired at court. He was however a rigid Calvinist, and had to take refuge at the château of Talcy after the St Bartholomew massacres of 1572. His love for Diana was a hopeless dream; they were separated by religion. He sang of his unhappy love in the famous lines of *Le Printemps du sieur d'Aubigné*.

Deeply affected by the separation, he apparently tried to commit suicide. Ambroise Paré, the king's surgeon, trepanned him on a table in the château after dulling his senses with eau-de-vie. As for the beautiful Diana, she married Guillaume de Musset. Less than three centuries late, little Alfred was born into the same family!

Above: The château's interior, with its 18th-century furniture.

Left page: The salon, with a gaming table; a view of the garden.

tour

A well, a dovecote and a keep

What is left of these thwarted loves? A well with a rose bush, Cassandra's famous rose bush as sung by Ronsard, the dovecote with its 1,500 pigeonholes, a winepress still needs to men to produce ten barrels of juice in one pressing. There is also the charm of a château of somewhat rustic appearance, providing the perfect setting for such beautiful roses. The château of Talcy is an integral part of the little village in the Beauce.

The square 15th-century keep used to be flanked by four hexagonal corner towers. The west wing has disappeared, but the east wing is still there, and extends back at right angles alongside the church. There used to be an elegant arched gallery, painted red like in the palaces of the Italian Renaissance. The interior of the château still has its fine 17th- and 18th-century furniture, and four Aubusson tapestries in the grand salon.
You should also see the room occupied by Catherine de Medici when she stayed at Talcy in 1562 with Charles IX and Henri of Navarre.

Above: The 16th-century dovecote, with its 1500 pigeonholes.

Anne de Pisseleu

The most beautiful of learned ladies: Chambord

If just one out of all the queens of Chambord had to be singled out, it would surely be Anne de Pisseleu, the blond lady-in-waiting to the king's mother, Louise of Savoy. François I met her in 1526 when he returned from captivity after his defeat at Pavia. Allied with Admiral Chabot, she reigned over both the court and the king's heart for twenty years, at odds with the Constable Anne de Montmorency. She was called "the most beautiful of learned ladies and the most learned of beautiful ladies". François I raised her to the rank of Duchess of Étampes. She genuinely adored him, and she alone accompanied him as he was dying of syphilis.

The dream of a megalomaniac king

Why Chambord? Why have chosen the site of a little manor used as a hunting lodge by the counts of Blois? Especially as in the autumn it was supposed to be haunted at night by the evil black huntsman. Like Versailles, Chambord was the result of a king's will. François I had just turned 25, and he enjoyed the place's abundant game and its location, not far from his good friend the Countess of Thouin, who had cared for him after a riding

CHAMBORD

The lantern of the double-spiral staircase leading to all the floors and the terraces. It is topped by a fleur-de-lis.

accident. On his return from Italy in 1519 he decided to build a château there, commensurate with his lack of moderation: "Such is my good pleasure" he was wont to say.

It was to be his life's work. He even planned to divert the Loire for the château's moats and basins, though in the end a stream, the Cosson, proved adequate. Enormous sums of money were spent. Thousands of workers toiled day and night. Marsh land had to be reclaimed, piles to be sunk for the foundations, a 32-km. wall to be built round the 5,000 hectares of the grounds. Work was interrupted several times, and lasted in all for twenty-five years. Even so, in 1547, at the death of the king Chambord was not finished. Who was really the architect? Leonardo da Vinci is often mentioned; he lived nearby, at the Clos-Lucé. So is Dominique of Cortona, known as Il Boccadoro, who had built a wooden model of the château. Did he use plans drawn up by Leonardo da Vinci? There is certainly a clear Italian influence, for even the structure of the keep is very similar to that of St Peter, in Rome. One name is forever linked to the gigantic enterprise: that of Jean Le Breton, who handled the finances of building Chambord – and who took advantage of the situation to build his own châteaux at Villesavin and Villandry.

The François I open staircase seen from the outside.

CHAMBORD

AN ITINERANT COURT

The court only stayed at Chambord long enough for a feast or a hunt. The furniture arrived first: hangings, tapestries to put some warmth into the cold walls of the enormous château. Beds with curtains and horsehair mattresses were laid next to the fireplaces. Six to eight people went in each one, head to foot. Tables were set up on trestles. There were no chairs, only "ployants" (folding stools). No plates, but a "tranchoir", a sort of wooden platter. No forks, but fingers. Such was life at court. For the king: heron paté, roasted oysters. Melons from Italy were very popular. Blowing one's nose in one's fingers was no longer allowed. Picking one's teeth with one's nails was even worse. A new treatise on good manners, called Il Cortegiano, was now applied at court.

Pomp, ceremony and an imperial visit

Work on the château, which had stopped when disaster struck at Pavia in 1525, was resumed. The royal block's three storeys were completed, and the two-tiered arched gallery now linked the keep to the corner towers. A few years later Brantôme couldn't help exclaiming, "It is one of the wonders of the world".
And yet François I would stay there for short visits only. It was a place for hunting parties, and on beautiful autumn mornings Chambord would awaken to the sound of hunting horns. At nightfall riders and followers would throw at the ladies' feet stags, roe deer and wild boars to be ripped open in the reddish glow of the enormous fireplaces.

1530 was an exceptional year: the king spent a whole month at Chambord, with his beautiful new queen, Eleanor of Hapsburg, Charles V's sister. His first wife, Claude of France, had died in 1524. In December 1539 a very distinguished guest was expected. Everything – the four hundred and forty rooms, eighty-three staircases, three hundred and sixty-five windows and eight hundred capitals – had to be readied for the arrival of Emperor Charles V. "Let's go to my place", the king had said with false modesty to his imperial visitor, who was obliged to admire the architectural feats and thousand and one works of art that adorned the château. François I was at the height of his reign that day, and Chambord was the ideal setting for the festivities. The king's fate, however, was already sealed. Unfaithful to his wives, first Claude, then Eleanor, he had been contaminated by a jealous mistress. The pox, syphilis, was to gnaw at him for eight years, until it finally killed him in 1547. In 1545 he stayed at Chambord for the last time, accompanied by the Queen of Navarre, his sister. He was prematurely aged, and it was doubtless in a moment of nostalgia that he wrote with a diamond on a window pane the famous lines:

> "*Souvent femme varie,*
> *Bien fol qui s'y fie*"

(Women are fickle, to trust them is mad).
Louis XIV, accompanied by the very young Marie Mancini, is supposed to have seen the lines – and smashed the window.

Claude, Eleanor, Françoise, Anne and the others

To whom were those disillusioned lines addressed? To the Countess of Thouin, or to his cousin Claude of France, who was more gentle than beautiful, limping slightly, like her mother, Anne of Brittany? He had married her when he was still Duke of Angoulême. She had lived a cloistered life at Blois, not far off, but not wielding much influence either, and she died at the age of 25, regretted by her subjects.

Below:
The grand staircase that spirals round a central core.

CHAMBORD

François I was taken prisoner by Charles V after being defeated at Pania in 1525; he recovered his freedom through the Treaty of Cambrai, also called the Paix des Dames ("the Ladies' Peace"). In exchange he had promised to marry Eleanor of Hapsburg. From having been Queen of Portugal, Eleanor thus became Queen of France in 1530. Despite her beauty, celebrated by Theodore de Bèze, the king neglected her, preferring his mistresses. She lived apart from the court, indulging in her two hobbies, reading and hunting. Childless when François I died, she went to live with her brother Charles V in the Netherlands.
Would any chronicler of the time have been able to list all the king's mistresses? Nevertheless, two of them strongly influenced the insatiable monarch's life. The dark corridors and secret staircases of Chambord were doubtless designed to enable the king to visit them. The first was the haughty and witty Françoise de Chateaubriand. She was certainly a woman of character. Married at the age of 17 to Jean de Montmorency-Laval, she became the king's mistress in 1518. Her "reign" lasted for ten years. Although she was criticised for abusing her position to benefit her brothers, everyone admired her panache when the king, having replaced her with the very young Anne d'Heilly, asked her to return the jewels he had given. She did… but melted down.

Above and left page:
The roofs of Chambord.
This forest of pinnacles,
pilasters and turrets,
with some 365 chimneys
and 800 capitals
looks like a miniature city.

Above:
Louis XIV's bedchamber, redecorated by the Marshal of Saxe in 1748, with a fireplace and wood panels from Versailles.

The second, the ravishing Anne de Pisseleu, was the true queen of Chambord. Although she was treated as a queen in the king's lifetime, at his death she was exiled and her duchy given to her arch-enemy, Diane de Poitiers.

Not the way it used to be

At the death of François I, Henri II finished the work started by his father, adding to the salamanders, François I's emblem, his own initials, linked to the crescent of Diane de Poitiers, his mistress. The queen, Catherine de Medici, still in order to pursued her study of experimental astrology. But nothing was the way it used to be. The château was falling into disrepair: the terraces leaked, and an inventory carried out at the time recorded the fact that all the furniture had disappeared. It had become a place of exile, as was the case for Gaston of Orleans, Louis XIII's younger brother. It remained however a place where people liked to hunt.

A pleasure palace for the Sun King

It was only under Louis XIV that sleeping beauty would reawaken. The Sun king enjoyed Chambord, to the point of having royal apartments fitted out on the first floor of the keep. In the autumn of 1669 he stayed there with his whole court. Hunting was his favourite pastime, of course, but there was also, "comedy, a ball and a grand supper, so that the court had never been so well entertained".
Molière and Lully put on a play called Monsieur de Pourceaugnac, which included interludes of ballet. "Lully, make me laugh," Molière had said The court applauded, but the king was visibly bored. Then Lully had the bright idea of jumping onto the keyboard of a harpsichord situated just below the stage. The comic effect was instantaneous, and the play was a great success.
A year later, on 14 October 1670, Molière put on Le Bourgeois Gentilhomme at Chambord. The holes made to hold the curtain can still be seen, as well as the little door leading backstage. The oriental farce was performed before the king in stony silence. The court was dumbfounded at Molière's impertinence. At the second performance the king was beaming with pleasure, and the play was a triumph!
The king had another château on his mind by then, Versailles. He nevertheless returned to Chambord several times, closely following the alterations being carried out by Mansart. Was there any point in this? The château was to remain unoccupied for twenty-five years, and the work was never to be finished.
In 1725 Louis XV offered Chambord to his parents-in-law, Stanislas and Catherine Leszczynski, the deposed sovereigns of Poland. The humidity of the moats and marshes was bad for Stanislas's rheumatism, however, so they went to Menars instead.

A marshal's baton for the hero of Fontenoy

Louis XV then gave Chambord to a talented megalomaniac, the condottiere Maurice of Saxe, who had been made Marshal of France after winning the battle of Fontenoy in 1745.

ABANDONED BY KINGS

This château, wrote Flaubert, "Was given to lots of people, as if nobody wanted it, or could keep it. It seems never to have been used, and always to have been too big." François I, during the forty years of his reign, spent only forty days there. Henri IV never set foot in it, Louis XIII put in only a brief appearance, and the court went there for the last time in 1684.

Horses, soldiers and women were the actors and protagonists of all sorts of intrigues, both comic and tragic, played out at Chambord. Louis XV had allowed the Marshal to keep his regiment of Saxe-Volontaires. Six brigades of 160 men were therefore garrisoned at Chambord, and the stables were turned into barracks. The Marshal drilled his men round the château to the sound of trumpets each morning. It was the first and only time that Chambord was really lived in.

A kingdom lost for a flag

This extravagant lifestyle ended in 1750 with the Marshal's death. Officially, he died of an ordinary lung complaint. In reality he was killed in a fight on the château grounds with the jealous husband of the Princess of Conti.
Chambord was ransacked during the Revolution. After having served as a garage for the Imperial coaches and carriages, in 1809 the château was given by Napoleon to his faithful Berthier, Prince of Wagram. When he died, his widow put it up for sale. The cost of restoring it was so high that a national subscription had to be raised in order to give it, in 1821, to the infant Duke of Bordeaux, the posthumous son of the heir to the throne, the Duke of Berry, who had just been assassinated.
This "miracle child" became Henri, Count of Chambord, the legitimist pretender to the throne of France. In 1871 a Monarchist majority was elected to parliament, and Henri was offered the crown. In October 1873 he rejected it, however, refusing to give up the "white flag of Henri IV". That is how the Republic was established in France, and how Henri V, through his own intransigence, was destined to remained no more than Count of Chambord. The last little joke played by history in this affair was the fact that in World War I the Counts' heirs, the Princes of Bourbon-Parme, chose to serve in the Austrian army! The Republic bore no grudge, magnanimously purchasing Chambord in 1932.

tour

The most sumptuous of the Loire châteaux

To reach the château you must penetrate deep into the grounds, a superb 5,000-hectare state forest enclosed by a 32-km. wall, with six gates corresponding to the six main avenues.
When, rounding a bend, Chambord suddenly appears in the glory of its white stone, the visitor is transfixed, petrified by the unreal, dream-like magnificence of the vision. So this is Chambord, the most grandiose, the most majestic, the most sumptuous of all the châteaux of the Loire. With its impressive 230-metre façade, surely only Versailles can equal it.

Four enormous towers flank the grandiose symmetrical façade. The quadrangular keep stands in the centre, with its four corner towers. The château itself has four hundred and forty rooms, eighty-three staircases, including thirteen main ones, three hundred and sixty-five windows and innumerable galleries linking the main parts of the building together.
Inside the keep you will find the famous, open, double-spiral staircase, in which people can go up and down without meeting. It ends with a 32-m. lantern, topped by a fleur-de-lis. This masterpiece of Renaissance art is said to have been designed by Leonardo da Vinci.

The keep itself is composed of thirty-two identical five-room apartments. Louis XIV's apartment is on the first floor, with wood panelling from Versailles and Gobelins tapestries. It was also occupied by Stanislas Leszczynski and the Marshal of Saxe.
François I's apartment is in the annexes to the east, and can be reached by galleries. The chapel, finished by Jules Hardouin-Mansart under Louis XIV, is in the northwest tower. The vault is adorned with suns, Louis's emblem. The stained-glass windows were commissioned by the Count of Chambord in the 19th century.

A fairy-tale roof terrace

The terraces form a miniature city, a forest of carved stone gables, dormers, chimneys and pinnacles under the 32-metre-high lantern. They form an extraordinary crown for the château. For Chateaubriand they evoked "an arabesque, a woman with her hair uplifted by an ascending wind". The rooftops of Chambord are magical indeed, a slate-coloured symphony of terraces, belvederes, lanterns, pinnacles, pilastered chimneys, dormers and battlements.

Chambord is the largest game reserve in France, with seven hundred cervidae and over a thousand wild boars. (Visitors are allowed in the western part only, where watchtowers have been set up). The village of Chambord, with its church, is unique in France, because it is entirely owned by the state. The inhabitants can only be tenants, and even the cemetery concessions belong not to the families, but to the state.

Above:
A general view of the château on a frosty morning.

Left-hand page:
The double-spiral staircase in its open tower, the château's most spectacular architectural achievement.

Anne or Léonor

Two women in charge: Villesavin

The news must have made quite a sensation: in 1545 François I put a woman — Anne Gedouin, widow of Jean Le Breton, the owner of Villesavin — in charge of "all estimates and contracts pertaining to the construction of Chambord". This was a major undertaking, involving what was probably one of the largest construction projects in the kingdom! He went even further, appointing Léonor, the daughter of the same Jean Le Breton, "Governor of the houses, château and buildings of Chambord", with of course "charge, garde et conciergerie".

A pied-à-terre near Chambord

The château stands on the site of a former seigniory, which in the early 14th century had belonged to Guy de Chatillon, Count of Blois. Like many other châteaux of the Loire, Villesavin was built by a prominent state official, who had become wealthy in the service of the king. Such was the case of Jean Le Breton. Like Robertet at Blois, Briçonnet and Bohier at Chenonceau, Berthelot at Azay-le-Rideau, or the unfortunate Semblançay, who, having

The marble basin in the courtyard; an Italian work of the early 16th century.

overstepped the mark ended up by being hanged at Montfaucon, Le Breton was in the service of the monarch. François I noticed him when he was still president of the Accounting Chamber at Blois, and made him Financial Controller of the gigantic Chambord project.

Work on the château was slow, however, for the good reason that Jean Le Breton wanted, for the sake of convenience, to have his own pied-à-terre close by. And as he offered better wages than the king… From 1537 onwards, therefore, Florentine workers, the very ones who had been hired to work on the royal constructions, built Villesavin. Who paid? Nobody knows, but the roofing, which is slate at present but which used to be lead (later requisitioned by Napoleon), came from Chambord.

A title of nobility

The presence behind the château of a dovecote (with an impressive timber frame) proves, if proof were required, that Le Breton had been ennobled as a reward for his services. The fifteen hundred pigeon-holes, reached by a revolving ladder (the droppings were used as fertiliser), give an approximate idea of the extent of the domain, each pigeon-hole corresponding to a precise area. The total here would be 1,000 hectares (2,500 acres). François I liked to stop at Villesavin, which can be taken as a mark of gratitude for services rendered by the financier.

"All the window-panes were made of crystal, and next to them there were paintings depicting Ovid's *Metamorphoses* and the coats-of-arms of all the Lords at the court of François I", writes a contemporary.

Jean Le Breton received the supreme honour of being made Controller General of the army.

Today Villesavin belongs to the Countess of Sparre and her family. It took thirty years to restore the château, step by step, to its Renaissance authenticity.

The impressive timber frame of the 16th-century dovecote, with its revolving ladder.

tour

Florentine grace

Somewhat lost on the green banks of the Beuvron between Chambord and Cheverny, Villesavin suffers from the proximity of its two illustrious neighbours. And yet this delightful little château, with its very Italian gracefulness, has a lot of charm. The low walls and tall roofs with their fine dormer windows adorned with carved pediments have seemingly human proportions. This fine residence, composed of a central block flanked by two symmetrical pavilions, has a large Florentine basin in white Carrare marble in the centre of the courtyard.

The series of terracotta medallions on the façade of the left wing represent the Caesars, doubtless as a reminder of the Roman origins of Villesavin: the *Villa Sabinus*, on Hadrian's Roman road. A remarkable collection of wedding costumes and since 1840 is also on display, and there is a curious museum of horse-drawn vehicles and children's perambulators. A living museum of carthorses runs from Easter to All Saints' day.

Left: The courtyard.

Above: Terracotta medallions, representing the Caesars, on the façade of the château's left wing.

Marie de Médici

The three queens: Blois

Just imagine the scene: a Queen of France suspended in mid-air! Despite her ample size, Marie de Medici, widow of Henri IV and mother of Louis XIII, had climbed over the balustrade of her window and begun to descend the steep façade des loges on rope ladders. When she at last reached the ground, she was dragged to a carriage waiting to take her to Angouleme. There she was to negotiate the terms of her reconciliation with her son, who was irritated by his exclusion from power. Louis XIII magnanimously accepted her terms, but the incorrigible Marie de Medici would continue to pursue her intrigues...

Amorous rivalry

There is probably no other château which has left so profound a mark on French history. Blois, the residence of kings and queens, towers over the Loire, which seems to recognise the château's importance, becoming broader in keeping with Blois' royal dimensions. For five centuries momentous events – some tragic, others almost comic – have taken place within these walls: stories of love and betrayal, births, deaths, assassinations and reconciliation; all amidst an exceptional flourishing of the arts. The name itself is premonitory, *Blois* derived from a Celtic word,

Bleitz, "the land of the wolves". They will indeed appear later! The remains of a roadside are all that is left of the Roman occupation. In the 10th century one of the first Counts of Blois, Theobald the Trickster, built a keep, which the Chatillon family turned into a formidable fortress in the 13th and 14th centuries. All that remains today are the former seigniorial room, the salle des États, and the tour de Foix, which stands in splendid isolation further south.

In 1392 Louis, Duke of Orleans, took possession of Blois in the most cavalier fashion. The owner, Count Guy de Chatillon, was very old, and his very beautiful wife fell into the arms of the impetuous duke. Being always short of funds, the latter succeeded in extorting enormous sums of money from his mistress, thereby ruining the old count, who was forced to sell his château… to his wife's lover!

Louis of Orleans, the new owner of Blois, had an elder brother – the King of France, Charles VI (1380-1400). The king was first known as Charles the Well-Beloved, and later as Charles the Mad, when in a fit of madness he killed four of his companions! For 30 years the kingdom was in a state of anarchy, which enabled Queen Isabella of Bavaria to hand over France to the English via the Treaty of Troyes in 1420.

The brick-and-stone Louis XII wing.

Valentina Visconti: "Nothing matters to me now"

On 17 August 1389, Jean-Giléas Visconti, Duke of Milan, married his daughter Valentina, to Louis of Orleans. No praise was too high for the first "queen" of Blois! She was cultured, sensitive, and elegant.
They had many children. But Louis was not a faithful husband. It was rumoured that he kept the portraits of his mistresses in a secret gallery of the château. He became the lover of Queen Isabella, who appointed him Lieutenant-General of the Kingdom. This led to a terrible civil war between the Orleaneses and the Burgundians. Louis of Orleans was assassinated in Paris on 23 November 1407.
The terrified Valentina fled to Blois with her children. She had engraved on the walls her heart's lament *"Rien ne m'est plus, plus ne m'est rien"* ("Nothing matters now, now nothing matters"). She died in 1408, but not before asking each of her children to avenge the unpunished crime.

The equestrian statue of Louis XII above the entrance porch.

The poet prince

One of her sons, the poet Charles of Orleans, was a subtle and refined prince. He had inherited the features and character of his mother, Valentina Visconti. He married at the age of 15, but lost his first wife. Obeying the promise made to his mother, he got some troops together to avenge his father, but met with defeat at Agincourt in 1415. Wounded and made prisoner, Charles spent 25 years in England, composing lays and songs in honour of young beauties.
That was how long it took to collect his ransom.
When at last he was released in 1440, the heir to Blois married the beautiful Marie of Clèves, daughter of Marie of Burgundy and granddaughter of John the Fearless. She accompanied her husband to Italy when he set out on a fruitless expedition to reconquer the province of Milan, which he had inherited through his mother. When they returned, they decided to live at Blois.

The octagonal well of the François I staircase.
"As finely chiselled as a Chinese ivory", Balzac wrote.

A court of artists and writers

The changes to the château that Charles had thought up in the mists of London were put into effect, but influenced by the wonders the two had discovered in Italy. The wing he built already shows the first signs of the Renaissance. The ground floor is a gallery with basket-handle arches. The brick and stone used for the first floor produce a sober façade, with mullioned windows and small dormers with moulded frames.
Charles of Orleans and Marie of Clèves gathered around them a court of artists and writers. Among them was François Villon, a disreputable individual, "as dry and black as a broomstick", who happened to be a poet of genius. He took refuge at Blois following the theft of the treasure of the college of Navarre. A strong tie developed between the ageing poet prince and the young villain. François Villon easily the famous Blois literary contest, in which twelve poets wrote on the same theme.

Married to the king's daughter

When Charles was 70 he fathered his last son, called Louis after his cousin, Louis XI. When the boy, the last descendant of the Orleans line, reached the age of 14, the king decided to marry him to his own daughter, Jeanne. She was a sickly and misshapen 12 year old. In all likelihood the union would have no issue, which would be fine for the French crown. The story has it that when Jeanne was first presented to Marie of Cleves, her future mother-in-law fainted. But the king's decision was final. On 8 September 1476 the Archbishop of Orleans blessed the marriage. Jeanne immediately retired to Lignières, where by royal command Louis of Orleans was to visit her twice a year, neither speaking to her nor looking at her.

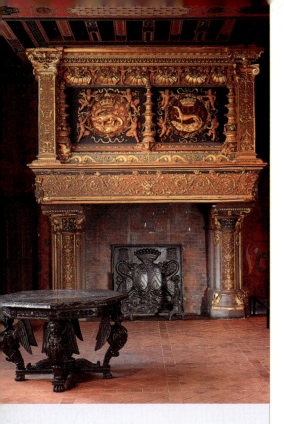

COURT LIFE

Anne of Brittany had three hundred people to serve her, yet she lived a simple life. She liked to wear velvet dresses with a Franciscan girdle round her waist, and she kept her hair in a Brittany head-dress. At 23, she was the first sovereign to live in the château of Blois. In the portraits Louis XII appears with a bonnet over his medium-length hair, wearing a short coat.

Anne of Brittany

Queen of France for the second time Louis was an energetic young man, fond of luxury and an easy life. He was also one of the best wrestlers of the land, and an excellent horseman: he could take a 5-m. ditch in one jump. Nothing singled him out for the throne, and yet on 18 April 1498 he suddenly found himself with the crown of France on his head. On that day, in his château at Amboise, Charles VIII (Louis XI's only son), accidentally killed himself at the age of 28, leaving no male heir. Louis of Orleans thus became Louis XII, and his days of frivolity were over. He has gone down in history as being both miserly and liberal, with a very good head for politics. As soon as he was crowned he took two major decisions: he chose Blois as his royal residence, and he had his marriage to Jeanne of France annulled. He had to marry Charles VIII's widow, Anne of Brittany, in order not to lose the Duchy of Brittany.

Poor Jeanne! By decree of Pope Alexander VI she was purely and simply repudiated. She took refuge at Bourges, where in 1501 she founded a religious order, the Annonciade. She was beatified in 1743 by Benedict XIV and canonised in 1950 by Pius XII.

Mother-in-law to François I

Anne of Brittany was twenty-two when she left Amboise for Blois to become queen for the second time. Louis XII spent 10 years making alterations to the château where he had spent his childhood, adding the northeast wing. François de Pontbriant and the architects who had built Amboise were in charge. The St Calais chapel was built in the pure Flamboyant style, and the Italian Pacello de Mercoliano laid out the terraced gardens, which were larger then, linking them together with the galerie des Cerfs. Anne decorated her apartments with tapestries, furniture, and gold and silverware from Amboise.

The strong-willed Anne clashed violently with the king over the marriage of their daughter, Claude. Her father wanted to

marry her to François of Angoulême, the future François I, while Anne preferred another suitor, Charles of Austria (Charles V)., She was obliged to give in, however, and the Austrian engagement was broken off.

Anne died a few months before her eldest daughter's wedding. She took to her grave her dream of an independent Brittany, which had hung for a moment in the balance of Claude's dowry. In 1534 Brittany was definitively attached to the kingdom of France.

Claude of France, "the good queen"

Claude married her cousin François of Angoulême in 1514. She was gentle and devout, not very pretty, and like her mother, she had a slight limp. In Blois she lived a cloistered life, under the thumb of Louise of Savoy, her mother-in-law, twice Regent of France. What else could she do? She carried no weight with her husband, a philanderer who was by no means

Above:
The States General chamber (convened in Blois in 1576 and 1588). It is 30-m. long and 18-m. wide. Columns with capitals divide it into two naves with barrel vaults.

Left-hand page:
The chimney-piece in the queen's apartments in the François Iwing, showing the salamander and the ermine.

Above:
The cabinet des Poisons, also known as "Catherine de Medici cabinet", on the first floor of the François I wing: 230 carved panels, of which 4 conceal a secret hiding place.

Right-hand page: Catherine de Médici's room, restored by Felix Duban around 1860.

discreet about his conquests. And yet in ten years of marriage she was pregnant seven times.

In 1515 Claude relinquished to her husband the rights to the province of Milan that she had inherited from her great-grandmother, Valentina Visconti,. In order to preserve the independence of Brittany, she bequeathed the duchy to her son François, the dauphin.

At the same period the king built for her, over medieval ruins, the most magnificent wing of the château, (the northwest wing, known as the François I wing), designed by the architects Dominique de Cortone and Jacques Sourdeau. They were also responsible for Blois's most spectacular masterpiece, the octagonal tower with its famous spiral staircase. Projecting from the façade, it was once in the middle of it. Balzac remarked that it was "so finely chiselled as to resemble Chinese ivory". It is large enough for a horseman to ride up it sitting upright. The work was finished in 1525, at the time of the Pavia campaign.

Claude, the good queen, had passed away a year earlier, at the age of 25, in her apartments at Blois. A sad destiny for one of the best queens France had ever had. Returning from captivity, there was nothing to keep François I at Blois. His ambitions and expensive tastes made him prefer Chambord, and later Fontainebleau.

Catherine de Medici, the black queen

With her comfortable embonpoint and sallow complexion, she was undoubtedly the deceitful schemer described so well by Brantôme. Daughter of Laurent de Medici and Madeleine de la Tour d'Auvergne, on 28 October 1533 she married the son of François I, the future Henri II. Despite the beautiful Diane de Poitiers' considerable influence over the young Henri, Catherine managed to bear him ten children. In 1560, on the accession of her son Charles IX she became Regent of France. By organising a tour of the country (1534-1566) to present him to the people, she was responsible for the future king's popularity.

A STRANGE WOMAN

Faced with an enterprising rival, Diane de Poitiers, the main pleasure left to Catherine de Medici was the solitary exercise of power, but she also indulged in dancing, hunting and astrology. What a strange woman! When she lost her husband, killed by Montgomery's lance in a tournament in 1559, her grief was sincere, to the point that she wore mourning for the rest of her life. That is why she is known to posterity as the "black queen".

Catherine liked Blois. She had a ground-floor gallery added to the François I wing, keeping for herself the first-floor apartments overlooking the gardens and the town. Tourists still visit Catherine's famous *cabinet des poisons*, decorated with 237 carved wooden panels concealing secret hiding places which can be opened by pressing on a hidden switch!

Murder in the château

When she was evicted from power by Henri III, her favourite son, she tried to act as moderator between the king and the Catholic League in the wars of religion that were ravaging France. To no avail. Dark clouds were gathering over the fortunes of the Valois. The tragedy – the assassination of the Duke of Guise, head of the League, by Henri III, a few days before Christmas 1588, would be played out in the château. Eight months later, on 2 August 1589, Henri was stabbed to death by an avenging fanatic, Jacques Clément. In the meantime he had struck an alliance with Henri of Navarre, the future Henri: the last of the Valois embracing the first of the Bourbons. And so it goes!

The interior of the Mansart wing, with the stairwell ceiling.

Right-hand page:
The wing built in the 17th century by François Mansart occupies the back of the courtyard. It remained unfinished and Gaston of Orleans was never able to live in it.

A place of internment

The château now belonged to Henri IV. But the ghost of the great Duke de Guise was still too powerful for anyone else to want to live there. Marie de Medici, Henri IV's widow, was exiled there by her son, Louis XIII, exasperated with her political plotting. Sent to Blois in 1617, she spent two years there. Supposedly exiled, she was in fact interned. She decided to escape, with the help of the Duke of Épernon, on 22 February 1619, thus her mid-air escapade. What a family! Her younger son, Gaston of Orleans, will also be banished from the court and placed under house arrest at Blois. He arrived with his own private court. After all, he was on home territory.

"Monsieur", an inveterate conspirator, was also responsible for the most unfortunate addition to the château. It was based on a grandiose plan by Mansart, which would have completely altered the overall architecture of Blois. The southwest Gothic wing, built by Charles of Orleans, and the western end of the François I wing were demolished and replaced by buildings in the classical style. Luckily, in 1638 work came to a halt, thanks to Richelieu. Gaston of Orleans spent the rest of his life at Blois, with an ever-dwindling court. He died of apoplexy in 1660. The château was then abandoned until the Revolution, when it was used as barracks.

Right-hand page:
The superb façade des Loges. Above the two levels of loges is an attic gallery under the roof.

Below:
The view from the château over the town and the river.

tour

The château, which is built on a promontory, consists of four parts arranged around a vast inner courtyard.

Feudal period. The salle des États is the former 13th-century seigniorial room of the Counts of Blois. The States General were convened there twice, in 1576 and 1588.
The tour de Foix is part of the old 13th-century fortress.

Gothic-Renaissance period. The Charles of Orleans gallery (dating from Louis XII). The gallery was reduced by half in the 19th century. It has basket-handle arches supported by columns with fleur-de-lis and ermine decorations.

The St Calais chapel, built under Louis XII, has a fine retable by a pupil of Leonardo da Vinci. The nave was demolished by Mansart in the 17th century. The façade is 19th century, Only the chancel is Gothic.
The Louis XII wing (1498-1503), in red-and-black brick, is flanked on the courtyard side by a gallery linking the two lateral staircases. The first floor houses the Fine Arts museum.

Renaissance period. The François I wing (1515-1524) is quintessential Renaissance. It has two façades, one facing the courtyard, with mullioned windows and dormers facing the sentry walk, and the steep outer façade, which conceals the medieval wall with two levels of "loges" flanked by pilasters and an attic gallery under the roof. The Archaeological Museum is on the ground floor.
The monumental staircase, which used to be in the centre of the wing, is enclosed in an octagonal well projecting from the façade. Its architecture is Gothic and its decoration Renaissance.

Classical period. François Mansart built the Gaston of Orleans wing (1635-1637) where the Charles of Orleans building used to stand. The municipal library is on the first floor.

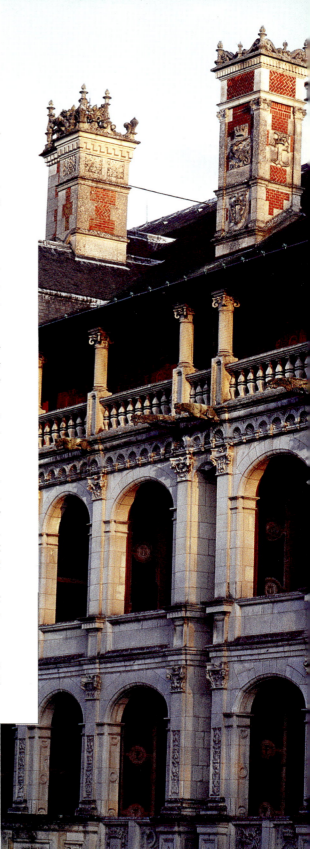

Catherine de Medici

Anne, Diane, Catherine and the others: Beauregard

Among the portraits in the *Galerie des Illustres* (Gallery of the Famed), observe all those women who seem to be gazing into the distance, in frozen contemplation of their past. Who is Anne of Brittany looking at? Charles VIII, her first, young husband who was mortally wounded at Amboise, or Louis XII, the father of Claude of France? And what about the cynical expression worn by Catherine de Medici? Is she thinking about the love of her husband, Henri II, for her arch-rival, Diane de Poitiers? Or is she looking at her sons, Kings of France all, and seeing their tragic destinies as a magician showed them to her, one moonless night at Chaumont?

François I's hunting lodge

This former hunting lodge at the edge of the Sologne was made a seigniory in 1455 by Louis of Orleans, the future Louis XII. The owner, Jean Doulcet, from a family of butchers established at Blois, had been ennobled in 1455. His son, François, undertook the construction of the first château.

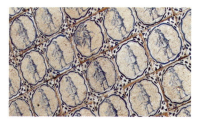

Top: The 327 portraits in the Galerie des Illustres, *with the Kings of France from Philip VI to Louis XIII.*

Bottom: Detail of the hand-painted Delft floor-tiles.

Beauregard was then sold to Jean de Thiers, Lord of Menars and Secretary of State to Henri II. He was a humanist, a man of letters, a friend of Ronsard, and it is to him that we owe most of the present château. In 1554 he commissioned the *cabinet des Grelots* (round golden bells), with its gilt carved-oak panelling by the famous Scibec de Carpi, who had worked at Anet and Fontainebleau. The coffered ceiling is decorated with the coat-of-arms of the Thiers family, with three golden *grelots*. It was however Paul Ardier, Controller of the Army and Treasurer of the Exchequer to Louis XIII, who enlarged the château in the 17th century and had the blue-and-white tiling for the portrait gallery made in Delft.

Two centuries later an extension was added to the galleries that formed the two levels of the Renaissance central building, with niches, a large attic and dormer windows.

Beauregard belongs today to the Countess Alain de Pavillon.

tour

The 327 illustres

Beauregard is admirably situated on the side of a hill overlooking the little village of Cellettes, but its interest lies mainly in its decoration. On entering the portrait gallery you will find three centuries of French history staring you in the face. In 1620 Paul Ardier commissioned the son of the Blois painter Jean Mosnier to paint an exceptional series of 327 portraits. They were all to be of the same size, in accordance with the fashion of the day, arranged in three rows and covering the whole of the room. It is an extraordinary experience to meet the gaze of fifteen kings, from Philip IV, who was beaten at Crécy, to Louis XIII, the almost absolute monarch. They are all there, side by side, obediently lined up in rows: kings, queens, ministers, soldiers, cardinals, popes, saints (male and female) – all those who held positions of importance or influence from Philip VI of Valois to Louis XIII! The 327 portraits have been eyeing each other ever since, in the appropriately named château of Beauregard ("beautiful regard").

There are also twelve symbolic paintings and eleven trophies. It is said that the Grande Demoiselle, who was passing through Beauregard, wanted to add her own portrait, but Louis XIV refused… In the 19th century Louis-Philippe had some of them copied for his "Musée des gloires de France".

The floor of the *Galerie des Illustres* is entirely paved with hand-painted Delft tiles representing an army on the march, in Louis XIII uniforms.

In the French-style park the landscape gardener Gilles Clément has laid out a garden, situated on a lower level, that echoes the portrait gallery: the "Jardin des portraits".

Marguerite

Love story: Cheverny

He was impetuous, irascible, ambitious, and was hardly ever there. She was young and neglected, left to her own devices in the four walls of a dismal fortified castle... The scene was set for tragedy. She took a lover to cure her boredom. Learning of it, he rushed back, killed the lover and offered his wife the choice between the sword and poison. She chose the latter. Shortly after, Henri Hurault, Lord of Cheverny, remarried. Marguerite was the second Countess of Cheverny. As in all the best love stories, she turned Henri into a contented husband and loving father. Making a clean slate of the past, she became the architect and soul of the new château.

A fortified residence

It all began with an old press-house in a place called Cheverny, on the edge of the vast Sologne forests. It belonged to magistrates from Blois. In 1510 Raoul Hurault, Chief Tax Collector under Louis XII, was authorised to build a château. The Lord of Cheverny became Viscount, then Count, and the family produced Secretaries of State, Ministers and Chancellors. It was Henri Hurault, Governor of Blois, who built Cheverny with his second wife, Marguerite, in the 1630s.

A TRAGIC TALE OF JEALOUSY

Henri Herault was in the service of Henri IV. He had the reputation of being vindictive and jealous, to the extent of shutting up his young wife, Françoise Chabot, in his castle at Cheverny. One day Henri IV took the liberty of making fun of the count. The latter, blind with rage, jumped on his horse, and rushed to Cheverny. The inevitable happened: arriving at dawn, he found his wife in the arms of another man. The lover jumped out of the window. Hurault finished him off in the garden, and then returned to his wife, giving her the choice between the sword and poison. She chose the latter.

C for Cheverny, H for Henri, M for Marguerite

In the early 17th century Marguerite, the new Countess of Cheverny, working with a pupil of the great architect Salomon de Brosse (who had built the Luxembourg palace for Marie de Medici), drew up the plans of a new château. It had great purity of line: a surprisingly narrow central bay, two almost square wings, with at each end a massive pavilion with a square dome and open-work lantern.

It was this perfectly proportioned ensemble that led to the classicism of Louis XIII buildings. Marguerite was everywhere, rising early, retiring late, the very soul of the project. Thanks to her, the decoration, partly the work of Jean Mosnier, a painter from Blois, was extremely refined. He did the coffered ceilings, the wainscoting and the chimney-piece in the king's bedchamber.

To her grief, Marguerite did not live to see her château finished. She died too soon, in 1635, leaving the count to finish her work. Sadly, he was alone when he signed the accomplishment of their lives' work with the interlaced letters of C for Cheverny, H for Henri and M for Marguerite.
In the words of their biographer, "Their thoughts, as united as their initials intertwined on the walls of the château; they approved the plans, followed and directed the building work, chose the interior decorations, without forgetting the parterre and the park."

An almost uninterrupted line

After Marguerite, the only ladies of Cheverny who have come down to posterity are two countesses: Marie-Johanne de la Carre Saumery, whose delightfully sensuous portrait by Mignard adorns the fireplace of the grand salon, and Anne de Thou, whose portrait was painted by François Clouet.
In 1764 the château passed out of the family for fifty years. It was bought by Count Jean-Nicolas Durfort de Saint Leu, a former Chief of Protocol to Louis XIV who had been ruined by the extravagance of life at the court of Versailles.
He became Cheverny's self-appointed historian. His first visit was a cruel disappointment. In despair he wrote: "The château is large, with five buildings, two of which are capped by a dome, but in all that there are only five rooms fit to be lived in. The rest is nothing but corridors in immense attics. Everything is in a deplorable state of disrepair, and my servants, who arrived before me, were up in arms…"
All the same, in the 18th century an elegant orangery was built in a secluded corner of the park. Cheverny weathered the Revolution unharmed, and under Charles X it was bought by the Marquis de Vibraye, a direct descendant of the Hurault family. The Huraults still own the château their forebears built four centuries ago. Thanks to such extraordinary continuity, Cheverny has come down to us exactly as it was in the Grand Siècle (the 17th century).

Above : 18th- century coffer in front of a Gobelins tapestry.

Left-hand page: The painted ceiling in the guardroom.

The château of Moulinsart

In the early morning autumn mist of the Sologne, the great drive leads up to a château that seems almost too demure for the Loire valley, which tends to be more marked by the Renaissance. But look at the façade, with its horizontal lines of stone, and the impressive slate roofs… without a doubt, this is Captain Haddock's château of Moulinsart, of *Tintin* fame.
In this "enchanted palace", as the Grande Mademoiselle used to call it, nothing has really changed. Cheverny still has its 17th- and 18th-century furniture, as well as the beautifully decorated panels and wainscoting, and the original paintings and tapestries.

On the first floor of the façade twelve oval niches, with busts of twelve Roman emperors, harmonise admirably with the perfect arrangement of the windows.

Upn entering the château, visitors cannot help but be impressed by the monumental grand staircase, with its straight flight and banisters. The date on it is 1634. Every single element seems to have been a pretext for sculpture. The auricular-style décor is one of the few examples in France of this type of ornamentation, which comes to us from the Netherlands. It puts the cartilaginous elements of human and animal anatomy (grotesque masks, sea molluscs, etc.) to decorative use. The most striking room is probably the king's bedchamber, with its exceptional harmony of blue, gold and red, the Hurault colours. The coffered ceiling painted by Mosnier tells the story of Perseus and Andromede.

The walls are hung with Gobelins tapestries dating from 1640, based on cartoons (life-sized sketches) by Simon Vouet that illustrate the Odyssey. The wainscoting in the dining-room shows scenes from Don Quixote.

Hunting at Cheverny

Cheverny's is famous for its hunt. There is a hunting museum in the outbuildings, with a trophy room in which two thousand stag antlers are on display. There are kennels next to it, with a pack of seventy hounds that are a cross between the Poitou breed and English foxhounds.

You may be fortunate enough to catch a glimpse of the Cheverny hunt and pack: the huntsman, the whippers-in, the grooms and the riders in their proud scarlet-and-blue coats.

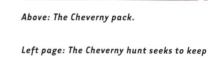

Above: The Cheverny pack.

Left page: The Cheverny hunt seeks to keep ancestral hunting traditions alive.

Madame de Staël

The "Empress of the mind": Chaumont

In 1810 Madame de Staël, nicknamed "the Empress of the mind", had gathered around her at Chaumont all the intellectuals who opposed Napoleon: Benjamin Constant; the seductive Madame Récamier; the German writer Schlegel; and a number of others. There was a lot of talk about politics, rumours, and a lot of writing, too. But there was one game that the little society, in its exile from Paris, enjoyed above all: the "private post". Everyone had to send a letter to another person at the château, and the recipient had to answer. It is easy to imagine the number of amorous intrigues that must have flourished thus!

The bald mountain

In the 10th century Eudes I, Count of Blois, considering that it would be a good place to build a castle, burnt the hill down to clear the land. Hence the name: *clavus mons* ("bald mountain"), "mont chauve", Chaumont. The story of Chaumont is something of a legend. The first Lord of Chaumont, Gelduin, was in despair. He had no son, only a daughter. This meant that at his death the château and the fief would go to his son-in-law. And then by good fortune, a second child was born. He was named

Right-hand page:
The chimney-piece in the troubadour style, renovated in the 19th century. The arms of the Amboise family can be seen.

Geoffroy. But he was so beautiful and delicate that very soon he was nicknamed "the little girl". His strange beauty accompanied him all his life (he lived to be a hundred). Yet he was an excellent horseman and hunter, much admired for his courage and physical endurance. He spent his life on horseback, going without sleep and food. But Geoffroy never sought to marry, so that in the region he was thought to be a reincarnation of a mythical androgynous creature.

Construction on the site of the old fortress was started by Charles I d'Amboise but lasted for three generations, from 1465 to 1511. All that is left of that château are the west wing and the four-storey tour d'Amboise. Chaumont is the perfect example of the transition from the Gothic to the Renaissance, when people no longer believed in defensive warfare. Walls were reduced in thickness decorated, windows were put in.

Too close to Chenonceau

On 31 March 1550 the Amboise family sold Chaumont to Catherine de Medici for 120,000 livres. The queen did not spend much time at Chaumont. Like the banker's daughter she was, she was content with the 5,000 livres annual income. There was also the unpleasant proximity of Chenonceau, belonging to her archrival, Diane de Poitiers, to consider. Diane and Catherine's husband, Henri II, were lovers, though he was 20 years her junior. After nine years of marriage, Catherine still had no children. Did she fear being sent to a convent or repudiated? In fact, Diane forced Henri to fulfil his marital obligations, which he did with considerable success: his repeated visits to the queen led to the birth of ten children. When the king died after being injured in a tourney, Catherine was at last able to take her revenge. Diane was forbidden to appear at court, and forced to return the crown jewels Henri had given her. Negotiations ensued: Diane was to give up Chenonceau in exchange for the solitary pleasures of Chaumont. She left her initials, two interlaced Ds alternating with the hunting horn, bow and quiver, on the machicolations of the sentry walk,. What else could she do?

THE GHOSTS OF CHAUMONT

According to the legend, Catherine de Medici, who was very keen on astrology, returned to Chaumont accompanied by the magician Cosimo Ruggieri. It was said that he could read in magic mirrors. Was it in the secret room in the Astrologer's tower that he conjured up the image of her sons, all future kings? Ruggieri had said: "As many times as they appear, so many years will they reign". First Catherine saw, in a flash, the livid and swollen face of the dauphin, François II. Her eldest son died after reigning for only a few months. Then Charles IX appeared, fourteen times, and lastly the Duke of Anjou, her favourite son, who reigned as Henri III, made fifteen appearances.

Above:
The porcupine, the emblem of Louis XII, on the façade of the east wing.

Top: The armoury of the château.

Bankers and wealthy parliamentarians

Catherine and Diane were succeeded at Chaumont by bankers and noblemen. Under Louis XV, Nicolas Bertin de Vaugyen, a rich parliamentarian, demolished one wing, giving the château its magnificent terrace.

In 1750 Jacques de Ray, Intendant of the Invalides, established a workshop run by an Italian, Nini, who produced a series of terracotta medallions with portraits of all the guests at Chaumont between 1765 and 1780.

Madame de Staël in exile

In 1810 one of the best-read, most brilliant women of her time, was assigned to residence at Chaumont. The daughter of a famous Geneva banker, Jacques Necker, who had been a minister of Louis XVI, Madame de Staël, held very advanced political views, and had dreamt of playing a role in the Revolution. The massacres of 1792 put an end to her ambitions.
She sought refuge in her father's house in Switzerland, where she met Benjamin Constant in 1794. Bonaparte hated her, and the feeling was mutual. She embodied opposition to tyranny under the Empire. "She is a real pest", Napoleon complained, Her exile in Chaumont was ideal for putting the finishing touches to her enormous work on Germany, *De l'Allemagne*, which was seized by Fouché and destroyed as soon as it was printed.

Poor little rich girl

In 1875 Marie, aged 16, the third daughter of a rich sugar magnate, Constant Say, happened to see Chaumont. "I want that', she cried, 'I want it'. Mr Say duly bought it for her, for the paltry sum of 1,406,500 francs. Two months later the little sugar heiress married Amédée de Broglie. The pair turned life at Chaumont into one long party. Anyone who counted in the world at the close of the 19th century visited Chaumont: the Shah of Persia, the Queen of Spain, Edward VII, etc. Nothing was too beautiful or too grandiose for Marie de Broglie. Not Miss Pungi the elephant, a present from a Maharajah, nor the Comédie Française, brought in from Paris to entertain the guests, nor the gigantic fireworks displays that woke up the villagers in the middle of the night.
The state bought Chaumont In 1938 for 1,800,000 francs. And the poor little rich girl died in sordid lodgings in Paris during the German occupation.

AN EXILE UNDER SURVEILLANCE

Who could you trust at Chaumont?

Napoleon was on the watch. Savary, the Chief of police, had bribed the young chambermaid, whom Madame trusted completely. So all the correspondence and everything that was said was reported to the Emperor. He even fired the Prefect of Blois, whom he felt was too conciliatory towards the exiles. Madame de Staël never left for America, which she had dreamed of doing, but went to live instead with her friend Mr de Salaberry, who owned the little château of Fossé.

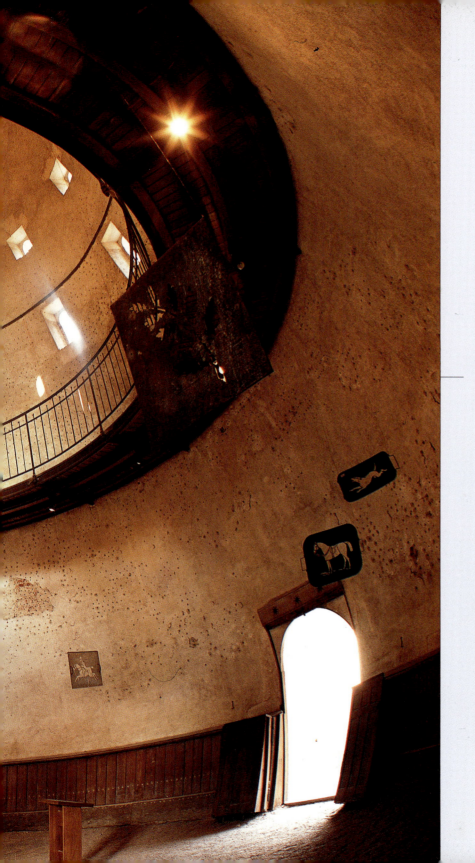

A GIGANTIC OPERATION

The Prince de Broglie carried out renovation work of Herculean proportions. The château was completely restored and refurbished, heating was installed, and electric lighting was put in (in 1898). Two hamlets were razed and the church moved in order to enlarge the 2,500-hectare park, which contained 38 km. of private roads. It was even rumoured at the time that there were flush toilets in the servants' quarters!

Preceding page: The old dovecote, converted in the 19th century into a riding school for the children of the château.

Right-hand page: Chaumont seen from the Loire. Below: Garden N° 9 at the International Garden Festival of Chaumont-sur-Loire: "Between heaven and earth" by Vincent Mayot and Thierry Nenot.

tour

Seen from the valley, Chaumont is a mirage, a citadel on the edge of a cliff in an immense halo of trees. It is certainly a Renaissance château, but the façade set among the towers looks very massive and austere. With its feudal air it dominates the little town of Chaumont and the Loire. The Gothic west wing, the oldest part (1465-1481), is flanked to the south by the impressive tour d'Amboise.
The entrance, with its drawbridge, is fortified by two round towers that bear the Amboise coat of arms. Diane de Poitiers's interlaced Ds, with a hunting horn, a bow and a quiver can also be seen at the base of the sentry walk. The arms of France appear on the entrance gate, with the initials of Louis XII and Anne of Brittany.

The Renaissance aspect becomes apparent after crossing the drawbridge, in the courtyard that opens on to a vast perspective of the countryside. The fortress aspect recedes with the delightfully light and feminine façades, festooned at the base with moulded garlands, arches, flamboyant balustrades and dormer windows.
The south and east wings (1498-1511) on each side of the entrance have clearly come under the influence of the Renaissance. The Council Room in the east wing has magnificent floor tiles that the de Broglie family brought in from a palace in Palermo, in Italy. At the northernmost end, next to the tour St Nicolas, the 15th- and 16th-century chapel contains a fine sculpted triptych and Flemish paintings.
The north wing was demolished in 1739 to make room for the terrace overlooking the Loire.

The gardens

The park, which was once to be enormous, suffered from inordinate felling that impaired the aesthetic quality of the site. Since 1992, however, all that has changed. Artists from all over the world now come to Chaumont each year to create extremely inventive gardens. In addition to the two large gardens, the experimental garden and the wild flower path, there is the Valley of the Mists, with plantations from Southeast Asia, and great waterfalls that cascade down from the top of the hill.
The International Garden Festival of Chaumont-sur-Loire takes place each year: 30 gardens left to the imagination of their creators. The rule is simple. On a given theme, each participant (artist, architect, botanist) is free to do exactly what he or she likes on a plot of 250 square metres each, within a budget that must not exceed FF80,000. May the best man or woman win!

Anne of Brittany

A young queen and a festive woman: Amboise

Amboise had never looked so beautiful as on 7 April in the year 1498. Charles VIII had decided to watch a game of tennis in the château moats, accompanied by his queen. The sight of the little woman limping by his side filled him with the same tender feelings as on the first day. For reasons of state he had married Anne of Brittany. The marriage attached the Duchy of Brittany to the Kingdom of France. Anne was 14 when he had married her, and now she was this strong-willed woman who spoke Greek and Latin. Thanks to her the Arts and Literature were introduced to the court at the château of Amboise.

A new *art de vivre*

Under Charles VIII the whole atmosphere at Amboise changed. From being austere and extremely constrained, it became dissipated and even insolent. There was a lot of singing and merry-making, and indeed visiting dignitaries were at times somewhat shocked. The king and the queen were so young! The two of them together created what was later called an *art de vivre*. In the portraits painted by the miniaturist Jean Perréal, which can be seen at the Bibliothèque Nationale, they appear astonishingly carefree.

THE AMBOISE LIONS

There used to be a menagerie in the moats of the château. When Charles VIII arrived at Amboise with his juvenile wife, he brought with him his hunting leopards, his marmots and his favourite dog. As for the queen, she had a passion for "estrange" little birds, trained to catch mosquitoes and flies. Such innocent pursuits did not last, however. It is said that in 1493, when she was seventeen, she gave live donkeys to the château lions.

The salle des états généraux, *rebuilt in the 19th century in the style of Charles VIII.*

Upon his return to France after the Italian campaign, Charles VIII settled at Amboise, which he was never to leave; he led a brilliant court life with the queen. He was described as being ugly and thick-lipped, with long, straggly hair and a red beard; he was in fact intelligent and well read. Anne had learnt to love him, with a possessive and terribly jealous love. She had become his ally, his advisor. It was she who had suggested that he should rebuild the fortress at Amboise, planted on its rock between the Loire and the Amasse, overlooking the slate roofs of the town.

The arrival of the queen completely transformed Amboise. Two extensions in the flamboyant style had been added to the Louis XI buildings: one, that has since been demolished, was the House of the Seven Virtues, in which the royal apartments were located. Anne was keen on hygiene and had had the first bathrooms installed. The other was the King's House. There was a tower at the end of each building: the tour des Minimes on the Loire side, and the tour Hurtault to the south.

The enormous project took eight years to complete. Work continued day and night, lit by torches and the red glow of braziers; in winter the stone was even thawed out "so that the masons should toil".

Finances were commensurate with the scope of the undertaking. Commynes tells us that the Amboise estate alone provided the king with an annual income of 1 million francs (of the time), and the "taille" (tax) brought in over 2.5 million francs. Part of these sums were spent on the construction of the "largest edifice to be built by a king for a hundred years", according to the chronicler.

The spirit of the Renaissance

The king had brought back from his Italian campaigns the heritage of the Renaissance. Not only were there tremendous amounts of booty that went to decorating Amboise, but twenty-two Italian craftsmen also landed on the banks of the Loire. There were stone-masons, goldsmiths, tapestry workers, the architect Fra Giacondo and the sculptors Guido Mazzoni and Jérôme Pacherot. It was as if Charles VIII had decided to rival the prestige of the great Italian families, the Sforzas, the Medicis, the Borgias. Unfortunately the work was too advanced for the architecture of the château to be fundamentally altered. He nevertheless had beautiful Italian gardens designed for the terrace overlooking the Loire.

A day of tragedy

On 7 April 1498, the king entered the Haquelebac gallery to watch a game of tennis. Though not a tall man, he bumped his head on a doorway. He stumbled, but managed to watch the first few sets. Suddenly "He fell over backwards and was incapable of speech". He lay in agony for nine hours. Anne, crying by his side, may have remembered that her marriage contract stipulated that should the king die without male issue, she was bound to marry the Duke of Orleans, his cousin and heir to the throne. At 11 p.m. all was over, "And so departed from this world such a great and powerful king, in such a miserable place".

A château for luxury and pleasure

Anne was only 22 when her husband died, but they had lived together for seven years. What a destiny! She had lost the dauphin, at the age of three, and three other children. And so on 8 January 1499 Anne of Brittany married Charles VIII's successor, Louis XII, who installed her at Blois. Under his reign, luxury and comfort blossomed throughout the country. The court had no fixed residence, as the king found nothing in Paris to his

AMBOISE

The tour Hurtault with its gargoyles.

liking. Consequently, many châteaux were built or enlarged in the Loire valley.

Amboise later became the residence of François of Angouleme and his mother, Louise of Savoy. The future François I received quite an education there. Amboise still remembers the innumerable festivities enjoyed by a court on which luxury and pleasures of all kinds– masquerades, balls, tournaments, prostitutes – were lavished on every occasion royal betrothals and births, departures for war, etc.

Hanged from the balconies

Amboise however soon seemed too small for a young and impetuous king, already intent on building Chambord. And then the dark times of the Wars of Religion fell upon the palace. François I had initially adopted a tolerant attitude towards the Reformation and the Protestants, but on 18 October 1534 the king discovered a violent tract against the abuses of the papal Mass posted by the Huguenots near the door of his room.

History, apparently, would not leave the château alone. In March, 1560 tragedy struck again with the famous "Amboise conspiracy". The plan was to kidnap the young King François II to remove him from the influence of the Guise family (his wife's uncles), who applied the anti-Protestant edicts with utmost rigour. The plot failed, and ended in a bloodbath. The bodies of the conspirators were strung from the balconies, under the curious eyes of the sovereign and the court who, despite the pestilential smell, came to watch the martyrdom of the Huguenots. After those dramatic events, royalty avoided Amboise, with its unpleasant memories. Louis XIII went there only to hunt, and Louis XIV turned the château into a prison. Fouquet, the Finance Minister, and Lauzun, a great womaniser who had seduced the "Grande Mademoiselle", were among the inmates.

Under the Directoire, part of the château was demolished, for lack of funds.

It was also used as a prison for Abdelkader (1848-1852), before belonging to the pretender to the throne of France.

Above: The balcony from which the Amboise conspirators were hanged in 1560.

Right-hand page:
The vaulting of the St Hubert chapel, a masterpiece of Gothic art.

tour

A small part of the original château

Set upon a rock between the Loire and the Amasse, the château of Amboise offers one of the finest views of the whole of the valley. From the terrace it is possible to see the Clos-Lucé to the southeast. Only a fifth of the edifice built by Charles VIII and Louis XII remains. All the rest is 19th century. Entrance to the château is through a vaulted passage leading to a terrace, which in the time of Charles VIII was completely surrounded by buildings. It is there that all the festivities took place.
Two enormous towers, 20 metres in diameter, flank the upper terrace. To the north stands the tour des Minimes, which was the original entrance to the château. It is crowned with a double terrace with battlements, built in the 19th century. It is famous for its ramp, which spirals up round an empty core, nine metres in diameter, and is wide enough for several horsemen to ride up side by side. To the south, the tour Hurtault is practically as it was when it was built in the late 15th century.

The St Hubert chapel, whose apse projects from the ramparts, is a masterpiece of flamboyant Gothic art, decorated by Flemish artists. Under a tombstone are supposed to lie the remains of Leonardo da Vinci. The chapel used to be part of the queen's apartments and served as her oratory. The original stained-glass windows were destroyed in 1940, and have been replaced by modern ones depicting scenes from the life of St Louis.
The *Logis du roi* (the King's House), overlooking the Loire, was built by Charles VIII in the Gothic style. The *salle des états généraux* (States General room), on the upper level, was restored in the early 20th century. It is built in stone and brick, and is divided into two naves with four pillars delicately ornamented with fleur-de-lys and ermine. It is there that the 1560 conspirators were judged and hanged from the balconies. The guardroom below opens out onto an arched gallery. Two round turrets flank the Louis XII – François I wing, set at right angles.

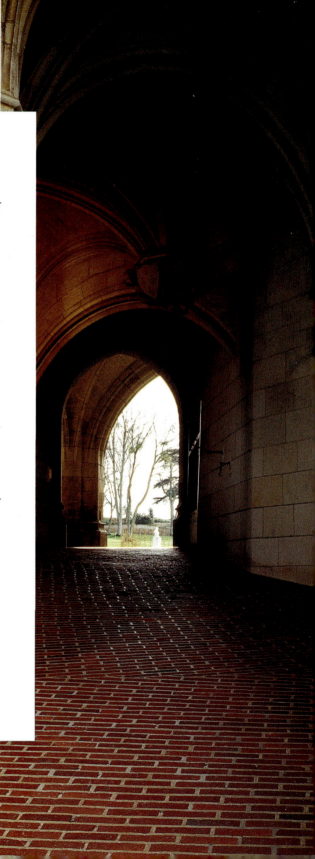

Right: The interior of the tour des Minimes, with its ramp accessible to horses.
Left: The St Hubert chapel, whose apse projects beyond the ramparts.

The Mona Lisa

The mysterious Florentine lady: Le Clos-Lucé

When Leonardo da Vinci abandoned Rome for the banks of the Loire, he took only three paintings with him, his three favourites. They were packed in leather satchels and carried on mules to the Clos-Lucé. There was the "Virgin and Child with St Anne", and "St John the Baptist with His Finger Raised", and especially the mysterious portrait of a Florentine lady. For a long time she was thought to be "La Belle Ferronnière". According to the secretary of the Cardinal d'Aragon, it was "the real-life picture of a lady of Florence commissioned by Julien de Medici". In actual fact it was the "Mona Lisa". When he died the artist bequeathed it to François I.

A manor called "Le Cloux"

This brick-and-stone manor house was built by Étienne Le Loup, Louis XI's butler, and then bought by Charles VIII in 1490. His wife, Anne of Brittany, went there at the time with the little dauphin, Charles-Orland, who died at the age of three. She returned there to mourn for her other children, who all died very young. Marguerite of Navarre, François I's sister, enjoyed the peace and quiet of Le Cloux, as it was known until the 17th century; it is there that she wrote her first poems.

A LEGENDARY DEATH

Contrary to what Ingres portrays in the picture painted in 1818, François I neither held a failing da Vinci's head nor caught his dying breath. The king was in St Germain en Laye at the time, celebrating the birth of his second son (the future Henri II). He was, however, moved to tears when he heard the news. The artist's body was borne by the chaplains of the St Florentin church of Amboise, accompanied by sixty paupers carrying sixty torches.

Left: The entrance to the secret tunnel used by François I to visit Leonardo da Vinci.

A young king under the spell of a great artist

In 1516, when he arrived at Amboise with his pupil Francesco Melzi and his servant Battisto de Villanis, Leonardo da Vinci was 64. François I, who met him shortly after the battle of Marignan, soon fell under the charm of this great artist and visionary man of science. He persuaded the old man, the initiator of the second Renaissance, to join him at Amboise.
What made Leonardo da Vinci leave Rome for the banks of the Loire? Certainly not the annual pension of 700 ecus granted by the king. Was it the charm of the young monarch, with his ambitious architectural projects? It was also true that he was finding less favour in Italy, with the rising popularity of Raphael and Michelangelo… It is said that the king, deeply moved, embraced him warmly when he arrived. He had reserved this delightful manor for him, at a stone's throw from his own château of Amboise.

A brilliant showman

Despite his severe rheumatism, Leonardo da Vinci was far from inactive at Clos-Lucé. He did not paint much, his right arm being paralysed, but he supervised the work of the pupils who had followed him. He was also a brilliant architect: he sketched a plan of a future ideal château at Chambord, with a telephone system, waterways, a landing stage, automatic doors, and even houses for the court that could be dismantled. He worked on a project for reclaiming the Sologne, while keeping the court fascinated with his magical illuminations and astonishing drawings of flying machines.
He was in fact a brilliant showman, and François I never tired of his conversation. He would crop up unannounced, arriving by the 500-m. tunnel between Amboise and Clos-Lucé.
Leonard da Vinci passed away in his manor, on 2 May 1519, when the construction of Chambord had only just started. That year the Loire froze over, and blocks of ice carried away the bridge at Amboise.

Above: Forty recent models of Leonardo da Vinci's most original inventions are exhibited at the château.

tour

The master's house

The Italian garden at Clos-Lucé, which slopes down to the river, is delightful. From May to December it is filled with the fragrance of thousands of roses. From the terrace one can see the château of Amboise.
On the ground floor, da Vinci's pupils decorated the walls of the oratory built by Charles VIII, where Anne of Brittany came to pray. Also worth visiting are the guardroom and the kitchen, which has a monumental chimney-piece.
The room on the first floor in which the artist died has been reconstituted. In the basement, which has been turned into a museum, some forty recent models of Leonardo da Vinci's inventions, based on his own notes and drawings, are exhibited.

Diane de Poitiers

A token of love: Chenonceau

Gaze upon her, in mourning for her husband, Louis de Brézé, as she was painted by François Clouet. The date is 1550, and Diane de Poitiers reigned in all her beauty over the heart of the king. What could he ever refuse her, when Joachim du Bellay had exclaimed: "God performed a miracle when he made you appear among us"? Diane, however, is above all a woman who kept her wits about her and knew how to manage her affairs. When Henri II, her royal lover, and 20 years her junior, gave her Chenonceau, she knew that as crown property it was non-transferable. The sale to the crown was therefore cancelled, on the pretext that the price was overvalued. Then all she had to do to become the legal owner was to buy Chenonceau at auction!

Catherine Briçonnet's fine manor house

Chenonceau, like Azay-le-Rideau, that other masterpiece of the Renaissance, was the work of women, the true queens of the valley. Catherine Briçonnet was the first.
She belonged to a rich family from Tours, and she married Thomas Bohier, the King's Tax Collector, who bought the Chenonceau domain.

Suspended above the river Cher, the château built by Catherine Briçonnet and the bridge built by Diane de Poitiers.

On 8 February 1513 he razed the feudal château built by the Marques family, retaining only the keep. Some little distance away he started to build the Bohier château, on the foundations of a fortified mill.

He was however kept very busy by his duties, and by the successive Italian campaigns. Catherine was therefore left to supervise the construction and embellishment of what was to be one of the first châteaux designed for peacetime use, leisure and festivities. Construction lasted from 1515 to 1522. Long before Chambord and Azay, Catherine Briçonnet made of Chenonceau one of the most beautiful Renaissance manor houses: a two-storey château of modest proportions, but graceful and light, with corbelled turrets.

In 1535, following a much publicised trial for embezzlement, the Bohier family had to sell the château to the Constable of France, Anne de Montmorency, a very close friend of François I. The king became accustomed to go hunting at Chenonceau, and on one occasion took his daughter-in-law, Catherine de Medici, with him. It was love at first sight, so François I gave the château to his son, Henri II. But when the king died, Catherine was forced to cede her place to her arch-rival, Diane de Poitiers, Henri II's official mistress.

A gift from a royal lover

When Diane de Poitiers received Chenonceau as a gift, she set about embellishing it. First she had to protect her château from floods by raising the level of the surrounding land. Detailed accounts have come down to us: 14,000 days' work were needed to build the terrace on which, from April 1551 to May 1553, she laid out her beautiful garden, a 2-hectare parterre in the Italian style. The whole region was put to work digging, planting, and building frames and arches for 14,000 hawthorn and hazelnut trees. Oaks and elms were planted along the wide avenues, hedges were trimmed according to precise plans. The end result was an extraordinary labyrinth adorned with fountains and basins.

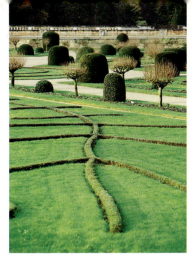
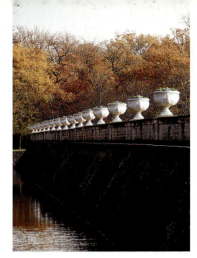

Above:
One of the two sphinxes guarding the entrance to the château, and details of the garden and park laid out by Diane de Poitiers.

Right-hand page: The grand gallery built by Catherine de Medici on the bridge built by Diane de Poitiers.

By the spring of 1552 she was able to receive the king and his retinue with pomp and ceremony. Diane also built the bridge across the river Cher to reach "a lush and woody grove, watered with fountains and green as an April meadow". She asked the great architect Philibert Delorme, who was in charge of all the royal buildings, to carry it out. He had already worked for her at Anet. Their plan was to build a two-storey gallery on the bridge, which would be the main reception hall of the château. Work began in 1556, but it was soon to be interrupted, for disaster struck: Henri II was killed during a tournament against Montgomery. Work on the château was brought to a sudden halt. Catherine de Medici, the neglected wife, was able to take her revenge. She would be the one to build the famous gallery. She also banished Diane de Poitiers from court and forced her to give back the jewellery and châteaux she had received from the king.

With a sad heart Diane de Poitiers left Chenonceau in 1559, retiring to her château at Anet. The Duchess of Valentinois (the short-lived title Henri II had bestowed upon her) was condemned to oblivion, but history remembers her by the name of Diane de Poitiers.

The absolute power of Catherine de Medici

Catherine de Medici, Regent of the Kingdom, was henceforth in sole command. It was she who gave Chenonceau its Florentine aspect, importing all the best from Italy. She designed the grounds, built the outbuildings, and undertook the construction of the two-storey gallery on Diane's bridge.

THE EGERIA OF THE RENAISSANCE

This Egeria, whom Clouet also painted as Diana the Huntress, had initially been the mistress of François I. He asked her to teach his son, the future Henri II, the facts of life. "Count on me", she said, "I shall make him my lover". Indeed she did. He remained her lover all his life, until his accidental death, despite the fact that he was twenty years her junior. Although a contemporary did remark that at 70 she looked 30. A witness also reports that, "You could never see His Majesty do ought else but wooing her, at whatever hour!" He gave her Chenonceau as a token of his love.

Chenonceau was her favourite place to stay. She organised endless festivities there in honour of her sons, the ephemeral Kings of France. Chronicles tell us of the arrival of François II, her eldest son, with Mary Stuart; the shocking masquerade when Henri III, returning from Poland, disguised himself as a woman, surrounded by his "mignons" and of the banquets, fireworks and naval battles on the Cher organised to celebrate Charles IX. Not to mention Catherine and her ladies-in-waiting, her famous "flying squad", whose task it was to seduce the gentlemen in order to spy upon them more effectively. The festivities and magnificence would not survive Catherine's death. But this great

The château seen from behind the gardens.
To the right, the tower built by the Marques family.

figure of the Renaissance – both hated and adulated; "both mannish and shapely", as Brantôme put it; wife of one king and mother of three more – marked the century with her vigorous action and acute sense of how to govern.

A cloak of sorrow and melancholy

Before dying in January 1589, Catherine de Medici left Chenonceau to Louise of Lorraine, the wife of her son Henri III. "*Ma mye*, ("My beloved") I hope I shall be well, pray God for

Catherine de Medici's cabinet.

me, and stay where you are", he wrote to her on 31 July 1589. The very next day he was assassinated by the Dominican Jacques Clément. Louise stayed put. The white queen (queens wore white for mourning) lived cloistered at Chenonceau. Her bedchamber, in the new apartments fitted out by Catherine de Medici, is between the library and the chapel. For twelve years Chenonceau was to live under a cloak of sorrow and melancholy. An inventory drawn up after her death speaks of "walls painted black, scattered with tears, dead men's bones and tombs". The only element of decoration was a full-length portrait of Henri III on the mantelpiece in the cabinet. After Diane and Catherine's festivities it is hard to imagine Chenonceau as a convent. Yet after Louise's death in 1601 a small community of Capuchin nuns moved into the northwest part of the château, with refectory, dormitory, oratory and chapter-house. This was the beginning of a period of over a hundred years during which Chenonceau would slumber.

A literary salon

Gabrielle d'Estrée, Henri IV's favourite, woke the sleeping château up with her beauty and vivacity, but Chenonceau only really came to life again with the brilliant salon of Madame Dupin. She was the wife of a Farmer General who had bought the château in 1740, and she received in her salon the literary celebrities of the 18th century, including Jean-Jacques Rousseau, her son's tutor. It was thanks to this exceptional woman, whom the villagers loved, that Chenonceau survived the Revolution intact.
In the 19th century a certain Madame Pelouse undertook to restore the château, with questionable results. The 20th century and the two World Wars affected Chenonceau indirectly: the grand gallery, with its black-and-white floor-tiles, was used as a military hospital. The same gallery served, of all things, as the line of demarcation between the occupied and unoccupied parts of France (from 1940 to 1942). Such is the march of history!

"L'ALLÉE DE SYLVIE"

Jean-Jacques Rousseau spent the autumn of 1746 at Chenonceau, the country residence of his benefactress, Madame Dupin. The daily routine consisted of going for walks and eating well, but also comprised music, and especially theatre. And indeed a theatre was set up at the end of the first floor gallery. He wrote a comedy, "L'engagement téméraire", and a little play that bears the name of one avenue of the park: "L'allée de Sylvie".

Above:
Catherine de Medici's formal bedchamber, with its walnut four-poster bed.

Right-hand page:
Diane de Poitiers as the Huntress by Primaticcio, in the François I room.

An enchantment from near and far

We are expecting it, we have seen its picture a thousand times, and yet we are spellbound when the château suddenly appears before us among the trees, meadows and vineyards. It is there in all its glory, bridging the Cher with its five arches and the famous two-storey gallery. At the end of a long avenue two sphinxes escaped from Chanteloup guard the entrance to the château. Before the drawbridge you will notice the vast terrace where the original castle stood, with the 15th-century round tower built by the Marques on its own to the left. The château that Catherine Briçonnet built on the foundations of a medieval mill, a pure gem of the Renaissance, is a large pavilion flanked by corner turrets. The windows are wide, with pilasters, the stairs are straight, in the Italian style, the first of their kind in France. The chapel and the library project outwards. The château leads to the 60-m. bridge and gallery built by Philbert Delorme, of which the sparse interior is relieved only by a monumental fireplace.

A rich interior

Chenonceau boasts an extremely rich collection of Renaissance furniture, with an exceptional series of 16th- and 17th-century tapestries, and paintings by great artists: Rubens, Tintoretto, Rigaud, Nattier… Your visit will take you to the bedchambers of the queens of Chenonceau: Diane's room, with the Flemish tapestries and the "Virgin with the rosary" by Murillo; the rooms used by Catherine, Louise, Gabrielle, and even the room of the five queens, Catherine de Medicis's two daughters and three daughters-in-law. In François I's room you will recognise the portrait of Diane de Poitiers by Primaticcio and the "Three Graces" attributed to Van Loo.

You will doubtless wish to visit the château kitchens in the basement between the piers of the old mill. They have recently been restored, along with the dining room, meat room and larder. In the olden days there would have been more than twenty kitchen boys, cooks and footmen milling around. A hundred and thirty copper utensils still adorn the walls.

Do not leave the château without visiting the royal stables, quite close to the gardens of Diane and Catherine, where you will discover the gallery of the Ladies of Chenonceau.

Lastly, the cave des Dômes, which you enter through the green garden, will be a very pleasant way to end your visit by tasting and purchasing the wines of the château of Chenonceau.

Jeanne de Perellos

The Scandalous Woman: Saint-Aignan

What a scandal it was! She was Spanish, and her name was Joan de Perellos. She was at the court of the Duchess of Burgundy. That is where Louis II of Chalon, Count of Saint Aignan, met her, in around 1420. He snatched her up and ran away with her to his castle on the banks of the Cher. There he repudiated his wife, née la Trémoille. He can still be seen with Joan, who became his second wife, on the walls of the crypt of the collegiate church of Saint Aignan.

The domain of Saint Aignan becomes a Duchy

In the 7th century two hermits from Saint Martin de Tours built a chapel dedicated to St Aignan. That was where Eudes I built the first castle. The following century Fulk Nerra, Count of Anjou, pulled it down. The domain then passed to the Donzy family, and then to the House of Bourbon and the Counts of Chalon.
In 1222 the inhabitants received their franchise charter. The present château was built in the 15th century, with its two Renaissance buildings at right angles and its octagonal tower topped by a lantern.
The owner at the time, Charles de Husson, and his wife, had an ambitious plan to build a four-cornered edifice round a courtyard. The idea was probably dropped when Charles de Husson died in 1525.

 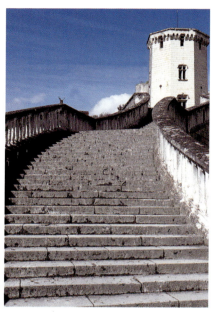

Left:
The château is firmly planted on its rock above the Cher.

Right:
The monumental staircase is still in use.

In the middle of the 16th century the new owners, called Beauvilliers, built the north wing and the west quadrangular pavilion. François I raised the domain of Saint Aignan to an earldom, and in 1663, thanks to Louis XIV, it became a duchy for the benefit of François de Beauvillier (1610-1681), Duke of Saint Aignan.

The château remained as it was, however until 1830, when Élodie de Beauvilliers and the Prince of Chalais, a Talleyrand-Périgord, arrived on the scene. They were both militant Catholics, so the first thing they did was to restore the chapel. The next was to build new stables, with a tower on top.

Over the course of years and marriages, the château adapted itself to the times. A large reception area was fitted out on the first floor of the north wing. It was reached by a monumental staircase giving onto the courtyard and a terrace. A pavilion supported by massive buttresses, meant to be in the Renaissance style, was built up against the old building.

tour

A monumental staircase

When you come from Blois, crossing the Cher over the stone bridge, the strength of the château's position is apparent. The long façade (admirably lit at night) recedes from the edge of the hill and extends endlessly to the left, until it runs into the porch-tower of the collegiate church. After that, there is nothing but the bevy of tiled and slate roofs of the little town, that seem to fade into the hills of the Cher towards Sergny and Couffy, with their clay and flint soils that produce such excellent wine.
Saint Aignan's church is a collegiate one built by Eudes II in the 12th- century. It is one of the most beautiful Romanesque churches in France, with its capitals decorated with monsters, hunting scenes and Biblical scenes. There is an impressive tower above the transept. The walls of the crypt are decorated with 12th and 14th- century frescoes: the "Descent from the cross with people imploring and praying" represents the lord of Saint Aignan, Louis II of Chalon. He is flanked by his mother, Marie de Parthenay, and his second wife, the Spaniard Joan of Perellos. You can walk up the monumental staircase that leads to the château. The view is splendid view from the terrace.

Solange de la Motte Saint-Pierre

She rode side-saddle: Montpoupon

To ride with the Montpoupon hunt! It was indeed a great honour to belong to one of the most famous hunts in France, founded in 1873. But time came to a stop here in 1939, when Solange de la Motte Saint-Pierre was 20 years old. The only daughter of the Lord of Montpoupon, the Master of the Hunt. As was proper at the time, she rode side-saddle. Today she is over 80, and in remarkable shape. She tells of days gone by, that come back to life on the walls of her museum: photographs, watercolours, hunting records, gouaches, drawings, costumes…Therein lies the greatness of Montpoupon.

A residence of the first Renaissance

In the 12th and 13th century Montpoupon was one of the castles that controlled the Aquitaine consular road, the future royal road from Paris to Spain. From 1320 to the middle of the 17th century the château belonged to the de Prie family, who were in the service of the King of France. In the 16th century Aymard de Prie, returning from Italy, built the entrance pavilion, which oscillates between the Gothic and the Renaissance styles.

AN ACTIVE HOSTESS

What a full life this woman has had! A trifle authoritarian, she certainly knows how to handle her staff, like her hunt. In 1959 she came to live permanently at Montpoupon. She created the "relais des gîtes ruraux" and the "route des Dames de Touraine", and in 1971 she opened her château to the public. Her greatest achievement however is probably to have become a great expert in silviculture, which is very obvious when you see her exceptional forests.

Montpoupon retains from its medieval past the round keep with machicolations and the defence towers.
During the Revolution the château chapel was dismantled and the curtain-wall pulled down. In 1857 the de la Motte Saint-Pierre family, owners of the château of Argy, moved in. A major restoration programme was carried out from 1885 to 1920.

Famous for its hunt

Hunting at Montpoupon had been renowned since 1873. The Montpoupon hunt was a fine sight, with its famous scarlet-and-amaranth coats: 14 horses, 80 hounds, a pack trained for stags; land and woods with neither limits nor secrets. The hunt was disbanded in 1949. Solange de la Motte Saint-Pierre's father died in 1956, the year when a hunted stag found itself trapped in the château courtyard. "It is a sign, when stags come and disturb the dead" she points out.

tour

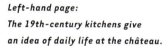

The third-largest hunting museum in France

Montpoupon is 12 km. south of Montrichard, at the crossing of several valleys, in an exceptional site surrounded by forests. The château is a residence of the first Renaissance, with the Marshal's room, the Amboise room, and especially the kitchens. The main curiosity of Montpoupon is the outbuildings, which have become the *Musée de la Vénerie*, the third largest hunting museum in France. The quality of the museum lies in its intimate character, its special atmosphere, and the numerous ordinary hunting objects.

There are twenty-five rooms open to the curiosity of the public: the huntsman's quarters, with its bedroom, hall, sitting room and dining room. The whippers-in's quarters; the uniforms, the Hermes room, the collection of old photographs and hunting horns, the artists' room, (Baron Finot, Henri de Linarès, Xavier de Poret, etc.); the reconstitution of the *sellerie* Dupré, (a Paris saddle-maker's shop), etc.

Left-hand page:
The 19th-century kitchens give an idea of daily life at the château.

Below, left: The reconstitution of a Paris saddle-maker's shop.

Below:
The window of the entrance gateway, which foreshadows the Renaissance.

Anna Branicka

Bunia Branicka : Montrésor

They were nearly all there: cousins, nephews, nieces and sisters-in-law, all escaped from communist Poland. It was just after the war, and they were the guests of Anna Branicka, Bunia ("grandmother") Branicka, as she was known at Montrésor. Anna was a Potocki, from a family of public figures, poets and writers, including Jan, the author of *Manuscript Found at Saragossa*. In 1886 she had married Xavier II Branicki, who inherited Montrésor. After his death in 1926 Anna took charge of Montrésor, managing the estate, and enlarging the château library. When she died in 1953 the name Branicki died with her. She had however succeeded in making Montrésor "a place of refuge for the Poles".

The grandfather of Diane de Poitiers

The first date one can ascertain in the history of Montrésor is 3 August 1203, when Philippe Auguste ordered the dismantling of the castle by letters patent.
The fortress, attributed to Fulk Nerra, had belonged to Henry II Plantagenet, Duke of Anjou and King of England. Montrésor then passed into the hands of the Paluaus, and the Bueils, who in 1395 began rebuilding the château. All that remains from that period are the fortified gateway and part of the double fortified enclosure.

Then in 1493 Montrésor was bought by the Lord of Bridoré, Imbert de Bastarny, grandfather of Diane de Poitiers, whose great achievement was to have been an intimate friend of Louis XI… and to have survived. For that "exceptional" king was fond of sending his advisors to his "cages" when they misbehaved…

Advisor to three kings

Imbert not only survived, but became advisor to Charles VIII, Louis XII and François I, and even frequented the king's banker Semblançay, who was hanged in 1527 for embezzlement. Being so close to the seat of power enabled Imbert to build the seigniorial apartments flanked by two machicolated towers, and to rebuild the village church. He wanted somewhere to put the family tombs. Then, through Henriette Catherine de Joyeuse, François de Bastarnay's heiress, Montrésor passed to her husband, Charles de Lorraine, Duke of Guise.

Montrésor, a little corner of Poland

In 1849 a new landlord arrived at Montrésor, a Polish Count, Xavier Branicki. He was a subject of the Tsar of Russia, but also a hot-headed member of the "conspiracy of 16", a group of young aristocrats who were demanding more liberty. His mother, Rose, fearing the effects of the Tsar's displeasure, had exiled him to France.
In Paris Branicki was a friend of Prince Napoleon, the future Napoleon III. He was actively progressive, frequenting Proudhon and subsidising *La Tribune des Peuples*. He soon started looking for a place to live, and decided on Montrésor. Xavier was a great art collector, and he had bought 25 paintings at the famous Fesch sale in Rome in 1846. Xavier was also an inveterate gambler. He lost a lot of money, but he also won a painting attributed to Veronese, "The Adulteress".

Above: the former St John the Baptist collegiate church, which can be seen from the château.
Top: the bust of the Polish ancestor

A wild place

Montrésor is very much off the beaten track, in one of the wildest parts of Touraine, in the depths of extensive state forests. At a bend in the road the château suddenly looms ahead, planted on its rocky spur. The 16th-century Gothic seigniorial building stands in the middle of a park, inside a fortified enclosure reinforced with ruined towers.

The furnishings, **chosen by Xavier Branicki,** have hardly changed since his time: hunting trophies, including an impressive 2-m. wolf; 15th-and 16th-century Italian paintings from the Fesch sale (Cardinal Fesch was an uncle of Napoleon's); family portraits by Winterhalter and Vigée-Lebrun; valuable gold and silver plate that had belonged to the kings of Poland.

Series editor: Evelyne Demey

Art directors: Caroline Renouf, Anne-Marie Rœderer
Design: Guillaume Eschapasse
Copy editor: Jean-Claude Dansac
Engraving: GCS
Printing: SYL

Photographs
by
Pascal Lemaître
and
David Bordes

We wish to thank for their help:
Agnès Bos et Xavier Dectot, the École des Chartes
and the owners, curators and staff of the châteaux
for their availabilty and trust.

© Éditions du Huitième Jour, 2001

ISBN: 2-914119-06-2